LEADER
OF
YOURSELF

TEN SKILLS OF LEADERSHIP

CAROL C. WILSON, Ed.D.

U LEAD PUBLISHING CO.
PRINCETON, NEW JERSEY

Cover Design by Christopher Wilson

First Edition

ISBN 0 - 9661537 - 0 - 7
Library of Congress Catalog Card Number 98 - 090429

Published by: ULEAD Publishing Co.
P.O. Box 2989
Princeton, NJ 08540
www.uleadpub.com

Printed by: The Print Center
New York, NY, USA

This book is lovingly dedicated
to my dear friend,
Phyllis Holden,
without whom
this book would not have been written.

ACKNOWLEDGMENTS

I wish to thank all those who cared, encouraged, and nagged me about writing this book. I extend sincere gratitude to Wilma Zoe Andrews, Joseph Bortniak, Joan Keating, and Anne King who kept me going when the going got rough.

Thank you, also, to my colleagues and the participants in my workshops, seminars, and speeches across the country, who urged me to put my words into writing.

A special thank you to my children, who have always believed in and loved me through the most difficult times of my life. You never let me give up. You are my inspiration.

CONTENTS

A leader is like a turtle —
to go forward you must
stick out your neck and
put your tail on the line.

Introduction

YOUR LIFE IS YOUR PERSONAL STORY

Life is a challenge. It can be exciting or dull, meaningful or empty. Whatever your perspective, your life is your personal story. How your story unfolds depends on the leadership skills you develop as you wind your way through each minute of your life. We all have experienced the desire to throw up our hands in desperation and look to the heavens shouting, "Why me?" The answer is, "Me because I am the leader of myself."

STUDY OF LEADERSHIP

I have been a student of leadership since I ventured out of our apartment in Flatbush to join others in play on the streets of Brooklyn, New York. The first time we chose teams to play stick ball or decided who would hold the rope in jump rope, I decided I needed to be a leader if I were going to survive on the streets. I needed to be in charge of framing my hopes and dreams. I knew I needed to learn about leadership. My thirst for knowledge about this subject has never been quenched. I still find the topic alluring. I not only observe leadership in people but also animals, in particular geese and deer, two of my favorite creatures.

My reason for spending a lifetime studying leadership is to find the answer to a fundamental question, "Can one person make a difference in this world?" Among the scholars of leadership the answer is a strong YES. History confirms that one person can influence the direction of a policy, group, culture or event. There is daily evidence of this truism reported in the media. There are leaders all around you making good choices—improving quality of life for themselves and others, spreading love to each person they meet, and most important leading happy, successful lives.

EACH PERSON IS A LEADER

You are the *Leader of Yourself*. When you think of leaders, focus on yourself instead of the typical leaders in politics, the military, sports, or the corporate world. Numerous writers have researched leadership qualities in famous people. However, the value of this ongoing analysis lies in our ability to translate these styles, characteristics, and traits into skills, strategies, and techniques that can be learned by each person in our society. This is a critical need because each person is a leader. You are the *Leader of Yourself*—the leader of the most important person in your world. You influence every person you meet everyday. You determine your quality of life.

THE MANY ROLES YOU PLAY IN YOUR LIFE—THE MANY HATS YOU WEAR

If you are feeling overwhelmed, examine the many roles you play in your life story: **family and personal roles**, such as daughter, son, mother, father, wife, husband, friend (this expands to a wide group of individuals, including confidantes, lovers, coffee clubbers, lunch bunchers); as well as <u>extended family roles</u>, such as aunt, uncle, niece, nephew, cousin, grandmother, grandfather, granddaughter, grandson; all the <u>in-law roles</u>, such as sister-in-law, brother-in-law, daughter-in-law, son-in-law, mother-in-law, father-in-law, and possibly even a friend-in-law.

Let's look at one of these roles in depth. The role of parent is comprehensive and includes caretaker, protector, TLC (tender loving care) giver, teacher, student, nurse, coach, chauffeur, and housekeeper. Each of these roles can be expanded to include numerous sub-roles.

Then add the **professional, career, or workplace roles**. These are numerous and diverse and can include student, worker, client, customer, patient, volunteer, club member, organization member, teacher and learner. Yes, you are both teacher and learner.

LEADER OF YOURSELF IS THE MOST IMPORTANT ROLE OF YOUR LIFE

Only when you are an effective *Leader of Yourself* can you function successfully in your other roles. Being a *Leader of Yourself* empowers you to reach for the stars in everything you do. It allows you to find strength when you face difficulties and challenges. It helps you in your many relationships. It strengthens your mind, body, and soul to assist you in living and treasuring each moment of your life.

Recently I had a learning experience in a setting where tired, overwhelmed, frustrated, stressed and scared people live:

I spent a day in a state prison in California. There were 4,600 male inmates housed in four yards with 1,100 men in each yard and 200 housed in a minimum security area. I was with a group that toured one yard. The tour was educational, informative, and gut-wrenching all at the same time. There was time for individual and small structured group interaction with the inmates at lunch, in the education facility, and in the bakery. The inmates who worked in this bakery were very proud of their product. They baked two kinds of delicious bread — white and wheat.

I talked with several inmates that day and forgot they were inmates, because when you interact on a one-to-one basis they just become men — some very handsome men, some very artistic men, some very articulate men, some very proud men. I also saw the other side of prison. I saw the angry men, the hostile men, and the con artists. I heard the offensive and vile language. I saw the obscene gestures. I felt the hatred. I sensed the violence and despair. I didn't have an opportunity to talk to these men, although I would have asked the same questions and probably received the same answers.

I asked several men the same question. These men represented the male population: white, black, Hispanic, Asian, rich, poor, tall, short, fat, thin, first children in the family, only child in the family, middle child in the family or tenth child in the family. I remember one gentleman who was handsomer and more charming than most movie stars. I remember a family man serving his fourth sentence, who was so proud of his four children.

The question was not difficult, just probing: <u>How could education have better prepared them to function in the world?</u> They all had the same answer though in different words. They said they liked prison because the rules were clear. They never had to decide what to wear. They never had to decide what to eat. They never had to decide what to do. They never had to decide even when to go to bed. No decision-making = no pressure = no stress = security.

These men said that many problems outside of prison started with little issues, such as whether to eat at McDonald's or Burger King. Sometimes these little decisions resulted in major conflict triggering actions that violated parole — resulting in a return to prison.

As a group these men said they never learned to learn; they never learned to make decisions; they never learned to take responsibility for their actions; and they never learned to express themselves appropriately.

INDIVIDUALITY

Each person has a different set of personality traits. These personality traits combine with a set of experiences unmatched by anyone to define the complex individual. This is our uniqueness. Even though each person is unique in this combination, there are common identified skills which are essential in order to effectively live life to the fullest potential.

IT STARTS EARLY

Many teachers label children either leaders or followers as early as preschool or kindergarten. Children then engage in activities in school that reinforce these labels, thus denying many other children access to leadership skills. How dare anyone suggest that a person be a follower in life! Living is a personal experience that must be developed, nurtured, supported and never relinquished to someone else. You are the *Leader of Yourself* even if you do nothing—even if you make bad decisions—even if you are not happy, peaceful or successful.

This lack of exposure to opportunities to develop leadership skills is a definite disadvantage to the child who is labeled a follower. This child grows into an adult follower. The problem intensifies when adult followers do not learn the necessary skills to be leaders. These adults then enter society knowing how to follow but not sure who to follow.

AND THE WORLD KEEPS CHANGING

The world is in transition. History tells the past. The future is yet to unfold. How different the world was last year. How different the world was before computers. How different the world was in the 1800's or in colonial times. How different the world was before the printing press.

Each person's total world was in one little corner of the earth. Perspectives were narrow. Communication was limited. There are times when this seems enviable. However, attempts to return to that time are futile. Time machines have yet to be invented—albeit they may be available in the future.

The world has shrunk. Communication alone demonstrates the change between the world of the colonists and the world today. Any doubters need only look at the broadcasting of war live. In our last military altercation, cameras welcomed our troops to the battlefield.

You may not like the present world, but it is your world. You participated in creating it. Each individual continues to participate in shaping the world every day. Even if you do nothing you still participate.

The knowledge base has been increasing exponentially at an alarming, or exciting rate, depending on your perspective. It should be an exciting rate because we are living in an exciting time—we are living in **now** time. Yet the number of individuals unaware of the changes in society is growing at a fast rate. In a one-week period, I had two experiences that demonstrate this point.

First, I had a conversation with a gentleman from the South who was developing a voice computer to assist severely handicapped people complete the basic chores of the day. This was a very sophisticated instrument designed to meet the needs of a special clientele. It was a fascinating discussion.

Later that same week, I had a conversation with a delightful older couple from the Northwest who were flying for the first time. The charming wife asked if they had "potties" aboard. When I showed her their location, she turned to her husband and said, "My goodness, they not only have indoor plumbing, but it flies!"

If you are not aware of the knowledge explosion, you are being excluded from participation as an active citizen in your city, country, or even the world. This can be scary. Some people retreat into groups such as cults, communes and militias for security and protection. Some people begin to live only for themselves and even withdraw from society.

THE FUTURE OFFERS THE OPPORTUNITY TO MAKE A DIFFERENCE

You can change your world. You can learn leadership skills that will help you take control of your life. The choice to improve your life and create a peaceful happy existence is yours. The world is ours as a group to change. It is up to each of us who lives here to participate in changing the world. We can change it person by person.

ANYTHING EASY HAS ALREADY BEEN DONE

If the mastery of leadership by each person was easy, it would have already been done. If the mastery of leadership by each person was already achieved by a large segment of our population, we would have a different society today. Start today to be a *Leader of Yourself.* Teach your children, family, and friends to be leaders. As large numbers master these skills, families, schools, organizations, businesses, and all society will begin to change because of *your* tiny but powerful impact on others.

This book focuses on a series of skills designed to help you be *Leader of Yourself.* Skills can be learned. We can develop them, improve, practice, refine, and master them. What are more important skills to master than those that will transform you into a *Leader of Yourself?* None of these skills alone will make you *Leader of Yourself.* It is the possession of all ten at some degree of mastery that will help you emerge as an effective *Leader of Yourself* and begin to change your life.

TEN SKILLS TO BECOMING *LEADER OF YOURSELF*

The quest to becoming *Leader of Yourself* is laid out in a series of **TEN SKILLS**. Each skill is taught from an educator's perspective, thus they include lessons. As you do each lesson and practice, you will inch forward toward mastery. Move forward at your own speed. Continue to move ahead with confidence. Focus on the positives. Focus on success. As you do you will feel your life begin to become more peaceful and rewarding, your relationships more enjoyable and meaningful, and your choices clearer. As each person moves forward, society as a whole will inch forward toward becoming the society we all know is possible.

The journey begins with **SKILL ONE: Learning To Learn.** This skill provides a key to unlocking the door to the wonderful world of learning. The myth that education is formal learning in a school setting is challenged. WIDENING YOUR PERSPECTIVES, CLASSROOMS OF LEARNING, BUILDING PORTFOLIOS IN THE MIND, and the excitement of learning are explored, as is the critical need for a *Leader of Yourself* to become a lifelong student of learning.

SKILL TWO: Learning To Build a Positive Attitude is designed to reconsider attitude as a skill that lies in the control of each individual. Because attitude affects us each minute, hour, day, week, month, year, and ultimately our total lifetime, it is essential for a *Leader of*

Yourself to know how to maintain a positive attitude in the most difficult times.

SKILL THREE: Learning To Communicate focuses on the complexity of communication from a different perspective—the PERSONAL FILTRATION SYSTEM. It is important that a leader have the ability to express clearly his or her wants, needs, concerns, ideas, viewpoints, and decisions. It is vital that a *Leader of Yourself* know how to communicate with others, thus contributing to the dialogue of the world.

SKILL FOUR: Learning To Love treats love not only as an emotion, Hollywood style, but also as a skill that can be learned. Mastery of this skill changes how you view yourself and others. This skill develops tolerance and acceptance of behavior while learning to control behavior. It is necessary for a *Leader of Yourself* to master this skill to build healthy relationships as well as to help solve societal problems.

SKILL FIVE: Learning To Focus Your Life inspires the focusing of your life by setting realistic target goals, planning, and evaluating your progress. This skill combines the ability to prioritize time (your most valuable resource) with the concept of vision, to enable a *Leader of Yourself* to make the most of each day.

SKILL SIX: Learning To Use Personal Power teaches the skills of reclaiming your personal power. Mastery of this skill can abolish addictions. Power, many times, is feared. Not to understand power is not to have any. It is mandatory that a *Leader of Yourself* understand and exercise personal power.

SKILL SEVEN: Learning To Create A Supportive Environment examines the skill of providing a comfortable, nurturing environment for yourself at home, at work, and in relationships. Mastery of this skill will decrease confrontation and arm you with tools to protect yourself in difficult situations. It is critical that a *Leader of Yourself* establish a personal comfort zone.

SKILL EIGHT: Learning To Grow From Adversity targets the hurdles, roadblocks, pain, tragedies, discords, catastrophes, and disappointments that life presents on a daily basis. This skill helps you face each challenge as an opportunity for growth. It is vital that a *Leader Of Yourself* knows how to replenish a PERSONAL TREASURE CHEST to be able to encounter adversity with the least amount of fear and trepidation.

SKILL NINE: Learning To Adapt To Change is probably one of the most needed skills today, due to the extraordinary acceleration of knowledge combined with the technology explosion. It is imperative that a *Leader of Yourself* have the ability to adapt to change at a comfort level that fosters excitement and reduces fear.

SKILL TEN: Learning To Embrace a Commitment presents the skills needed to accept responsibility to fulfill the commitments in life. This skill includes understanding, exploring, and choosing commitments at different levels and for different time durations. It is crucial that a *Leader of Yourself* embrace commitment together with responsibility.

ENJOY LEARNING!

ENJOY LEADING!

SKILL

I

Learning to Learn

SCHOOL = LEARNING = EDUCATION

This commonly held equation about learning is a myth. Learning is so much more than formal education. Learning is lifelong. Opportunities to learn are available from each person you meet every day in your environment. Opportunities to learn are available through many sources in your home: books, newspapers, magazines, posters, cards, the telephone, computer, television, radio, tapes, and movies.

Opportunities to learn are available in activities such as walking along the seashore, hiking in the desert, climbing in the mountains, swimming in a lake, fishing in a stream, skiing down a mountain, skating on a pond, strolling down a street, or riding in a vehicle. Many of these opportunities are available on a daily basis. Some are available at rare intervals. Some are available once in a lifetime. How many of these opportunities do you view as learning experiences or CLASSROOMS OF LEARNING?

• *LEARNING IS EXCITING*•

• *LEARNING IS LIFELONG*•

• *LEARNING IS THE KEY TO BEING A LEADER*•

YOUR TOTAL ENVIRONMENT IS A CLASSROOM OF LEARNING

We need to redefine CLASSROOMS OF LEARNING. For many young children watching Barney on television or tape is a CLASSROOM OF LEARNING. Captain Kangaroo provided a CLASSROOM OF LEARNING on television for my children for many years. For older children a video arcade can be a CLASSROOM OF LEARNING. Shopping malls provide a CLASSROOM OF LEARNING for many teenagers. If each activity for children were viewed as a CLASSROOM OF LEARNING, there would be more scrutiny in the selection.

CLASSROOMS OF LEARNING do not exist only in schools. This is a major concept in learning. There is a mind-set about education that has been passed down for generations, including the generations before electricity, telephones, automobiles, airplanes, and computers. Yet this preconceived mind-set continues even after these inventions have transformed our world into one that earlier generations would not recognize. It is time to expand the mind-set of CLASSROOMS OF LEARNING.

When you enter into stimulating conversations with your friends, relatives, and acquaintances, you are learning. When you observe people at work or play, you are learning. You learn from every person you meet and even some you never see face to face. You learn from animals, plants, rivers, oceans, mountains, and deserts in your environment.

I recently met a family from Alaska on an airplane. I did as I always do—asked questions. This time they were about Alaska. Drawing from my reference point, I asked about the cost of food in Alaska. Friends had said that it was very expensive. The gentleman informed me that food was readily available in the form of fresh salmon and halibut caught off the shore of the island on which he lived. The fish combined with berries made not only an economical but healthy diet. He elaborated with great detail the many creative ways to fix salmon and halibut. For red meat they had permission to bag six deer a year. They had also learned to prepare venison in a variety of delectable ways. My mouth was watering as I looked down at my cold wet sandwich served as lunch.

I then asked about crime or community problems that were prevalent in his corner of the world. I was absolutely amazed to learn that bears were a threatening problem for the people of the island. I further learned how groups of dogs were able to assist in running off the bears. Children are taught at a young age how to protect themselves from the bears because of the danger.

Our conversation continued as we discussed polar bears and how dangerous they can be to humans because of their aggressive nature. He related harrowing experiences with these magnificent creatures of the North.

This disappointed me because I had just visited the Denver Zoo and seen the two new cubs, Klondike and Snow. I really enjoyed watching them cavort and play. I learned more about bears in that short plane ride than all my visits to zoos. Upon my arrival home, I bought books to increase my knowledge about bears.

I could have learned an equal amount of information on different topics from others on that plane. Think of the knowledge about a variety of topics that was present on that plane. Think of how each person keeps that knowledge bottled up instead of providing learning opportunities for others. When I got off the plane I felt I had learned new information and understanding about Alaska and bears in a most interesting CLASSROOM OF LEARNING —a stranger on an airplane. What a delightful way to learn!

A PORTFOLIO IN THE MIND

Learning is powerful. You store your learning in a PORTFOLIO IN YOUR MIND. Each piece of knowledge you add to your portfolio WIDENS YOUR PERSPECTIVE and improves your ability to make better decisions, to achieve personal and professional success and, most importantly, to secure happiness and peace in your life. This is why it is important to broaden your perspectives and increase the size of your own personal portfolio. It is everyone's responsibility to teach others—when you teach, you also learn. There is a wealth of information in each person we meet. Each person can help another to build a portfolio.

BUILDING YOUR PORTFOLIO

We must learn to use multiple sources to build our portfolio: conversation; our senses—sight, hearing, taste, touch, smell; the media— newspapers, magazines, books, radio, television; the arts— movies, art, dance, drama, music; and sporting events, including individual and spectator sports. The list is too long to enumerate. Certainly we can learn something every minute of the day.

We learn from children. There are many lessons to learn from children. Children have an insatiable curiosity. There are lessons for adults to learn about curiosity. Children have an innocent honesty. There are certainly lessons for adults to learn about honesty. Children continually ask questions, many times to the point of embarrassment and annoyance. Instead of stifling the questioning because it is irritating, encourage and guide it.

We learn from teenagers (watch out for this group)! Teenagers are searching for answers. They look in different places. We can learn from their search and WIDEN OUR PERSPECTIVES. Their interest in pursuing new subjects and topics, their interest in technology, their ability to live in the present and not reflect totally on the past can all be admirable qualities.

One evening I watched a new program on television. I'd found it accidentally as I was looking for news. The parody was about Forrest Gump and Lee Harvey Oswald. They were together in the Dallas Textbook Repository when President John F. Kennedy was shot. They were distressed—they really meant to shoot the President's wife. I was appalled and found the program offensive.

The next day I was in a meeting where two very intelligent high school seniors were present. I decided to ask their view on the program. They were not offended and found the program humorous. They reminded me that it was a parody and in fact they viewed John F. Kennedy the same way I viewed Presidents Monroe or Buchanan. Kennedy was a figure from the past with whom they could not identify.

This viewpoint was a learning experience for me and gave me new insight into today's generation. This is learning! This is understanding the generation gap!

Later that year I had another wonderful opportunity to learn more about the generation gap and the mind of teenagers.

I had been invited to the beach by my grandson and his friend. These two teenagers are each over six feet tall and truly big boys. They were great company and we had a lot of fun.

I wanted to build a sand castle. They started to gather the sand and in a short time they had built a mountain with a plane crashed into the side and ambulances driving to the scene. I said, "We won't be building anything violent on my watch."

So I started to carve my own sand favorite, a giant sea turtle. My grandson and his friend really got into building the turtle and helped build a spectacular one. As children went by they were delighted to see the large sea turtle.

There is enough violence in the world. There definitely is a generation gap that we can't influence until we know its scope. I learned the scope that day. So did they!

We learn from everyone: children and adults who are rich or poor and represent all races and ethnic groups. Just imagine what you can learn from people— languages, cultures, arts, traditions, festivals, celebrations, trials, tribulations, and the list goes on and on... Talking to people is a wonderful CLASSROOM OF LEARNING and one way to add to the PORTFOLIO IN YOUR MIND and WIDEN YOUR PERSPECTIVE.

WIDEN YOUR PERSPECTIVE

The more information you have about the world and the more you learn to use that information, the easier it is to make decisions in your daily life. If you want to comprehend the wide scope of information and knowledge available, go to a library or bookstore and browse through the books. You will be astonished at the vast array of topics and areas of interest. You will also be amazed at how many complete sections there are about which you have minimal information. You may even find some sections that look totally foreign to you, and yet you will find volumes of books written about these topics. It is mind-blowing. It is challenging. Just to read all the books in which you are interested would take many lifetimes. What about all the books about which you have little or no information? Does this mean you shouldn't read them? You might discover you are curious about these topics and find a new area of interest.

I once had a wonderful opportunity to host a cadre of teachers from Japan. Their visit was an extraordinary learning experience.

On the first day these teachers met with school board members and administrators to discuss governance, curriculum, and other current issues of our educational system. The curriculum in Japan is usually described as traditional subjects interwoven with the arts.
I watched the joy of these teachers as they interacted

with children in the classroom. It was a wonderful experience to see these Japanese teachers on the playground swinging and going down slides with the children. They engaged in endless conversation with students and teachers even though they were a little shy about their English. There was no generation gap. There was no culture barrier. There was no language barrier. There was only a common bond of learning and love between student and teacher or teacher and teacher.

At the end of their stay the Japanese teachers held a reception for school officials. This affair was an incredible adventure. The elegance demonstrated at that reception was extraordinary. The scope of their talents included readings, singing "Red River Valley" with a Japanese accent, origami, haiku, juggling, spinning tops, poetry, sketching, crafts, and the most clever way of distributing gifts that had been handmade by themselves and relatives in Japan. When the evening was over, they formed an arch and we exited the room accompanied by another wonderful musical performance.

The wide range of talents exhibited by this cadre of teachers was impressive. Even though they all possessed different levels of expertise and talent in different areas, they all participated. They were not inhibited. They were not scared. They were proud. They were learners. They were teachers. They were thanking fellow educators for their warm hospitality. I was in awe!

ABANDONMENT OF LEARNING

Sometimes it feels as if there has been an abandonment of developing the mind. This is not a new phenomenon in our society but rather a cancer that has been building for many years. As historian John Lukacs wrote in his essay <u>Our Seven Deadly Sins of Misdiagnosis</u>, "The problem is not education. It is the abandonment of learning." Learning is so powerful, yet so neglected.

Each year young inquisitive children with beaming faces and hundreds of questions enter kindergarten.

Then, what happens to these children? Some eyes deaden to learning by third grade. Some eyes deaden to learning by eighth grade. Some eyes deaden to learning by twelfth grade. Even a large number of our university students have eyes deadened to learning. They do what is required to earn grades and credits for graduation. Yet they have neither internalized the excitement of learning nor experienced the thirst for knowledge. They do not treasure learning or exhibit pride in being a student of lifelong learning.

•WHAT DO YOUR EYES REFLECT ABOUT LEARNING?•

•IS LEARNING EXCITING?•

During the sixties, many traditions and institutions were challenged. This challenge was good for the mind. However, the very people who challenged the system did not follow through to improve the system by becoming lifelong students of learning. This has had many consequences for education. The system that was challenged to its very core and identified as needing improvement was further weakened when the knowledge base and technology accelerated exponentially at an unprecedented rate. Where are the students of learning? Where are the leaders of learning?

EMOTIONALISM

It is critical to develop your total mind along with your emotions. Particularly in our world today, we see daily examples of the exploitation of the emotions. Society in a rapidly changing technological time is missing the problem-solvers and decision-makers required to keep our society in balance. Therefore, most of the emotions demonstrated are negative.

Everything is aimed at our emotions—hatred, violence, sex, crime. Our senses are constantly being pummeled by negative visuals and audios. These negative influences are causing a major breakdown in individuals, families, and society. This breakdown is even infiltrating the political arena and attacking the very foundations of our society. This attack can be seen at all levels of our government.

A major influence in this breakdown is the media, which has become tabloid journalism, saturating the emotions with incidents of hatred, sex, and violence. This constant barrage by all forms of media can be likened to subtle brainwashing. Our children, our most precious resource, are not spared this constant flow of negativity, but rather are besieged by a violent and totally inappropriate use of vocabulary and pictures. Adolescents watch programs in which role models may boast of sexual promiscuity and the use of drugs and other harmful substances.

If you sample the themes of talk shows, you can clearly see the nature of the vocabulary and conversation. This saturation continues to overwork the emotional area of the mind instead of expanding the intellectual capacities. The result of this onslaught is a society where solutions to complex problems are found in simplistic emotional answers. A *Leader of Yourself* sees the danger in store for an individual, family, organization, city, or country where this becomes the normal behavior.

The danger in censoring the media is an erosion of our constitutional rights. A *Leader of Yourself* cannot support this type of media but certainly cannot support censorship. However, a *Leader of Yourself* can influence the media in the following ways:

- can buy newspapers that present factual information and stimulating in-depth articles,
- can encourage those newspapers to respect and take a leadership role in learning,
- can listen to radio shows where learning takes

place, where debates are informative and issue-driven instead of personal attacks and hatred,

- can watch television stations that present programs that promote learning, showcase performances, provide documentaries that are educational and informative, and air news shows that examine issues from all perspectives,
- can buy products and support the sponsors of those radio and television shows,
- can encourage others to help in the campaign to provide a better media environment.

The media presents what society wants—it's called the war of the ratings. We need leaders to tell the media what they want in large numbers. Do you realize how quickly and easily this could be done if each *Leader of Yourself* stepped forward to be counted? This has nothing to do with the political agendas of conservatives, moderates, or liberals. This has nothing to do with religion. This has everything to do with learning and the environment that is brainwashing children and ultimately society. This is not a complex plan, but rather a simple, low cost, responsible one.

• *NOW IS THE TIME FOR LEADERSHIP*•

IMPROVEMENT OF EDUCATION

The major perception about learning is that it occurs in the schoolhouse—commonly known as formal education. While the numbers of young people enrolled in formal education have swollen beyond prediction, our value of learning has declined. In many ways this is a societal problem and in other ways it is an institutional problem.

First, let us examine the societal problem. Learning is not valued. Across this country, cities are building magnificent arenas for basketball, baseball and football, while in many cases the symphony and ballet companies barely cover costs. These cultural events are not treasured at the same level as sports. When budgets are cut in schools, cities, and towns, the arts become the first victim. We tax for sports. We count on volunteers for the arts. We build budgets for sports. We cut budgets for the arts.

The arts are more than entertainment. They serve as a vehicle for overcoming prejudice, hate and violence. They are the difference between a civilized and an uncivilized society. The arts encourage free expression of viewpoints and ideas through different forms, such as sculpture, painting, music, and drama.

The arts reflect the mind, body and soul of the people of a culture. The more we learn about a culture, the more we can appreciate and relate to that culture. It is impossible to admire an artist's work or enjoy a musician's performance while harboring prejudice or holding hatred in your heart toward that person at the same time. And yet at the very time we need answers to eliminating prejudice, violence, and hatred, the arts—a possible vehicle for solving the problem—are not supported. We need to look below the surface to find creative solutions to complex problems. The arts and sports both serve as CLASSROOMS OF LEARNING. Each has its value. Each has different purposes. Each teaches different lessons. Each meets different needs.

**•ONE IS NOT BETTER THAN THE OTHER
—JUST DIFFERENT•**

Next let's look at the institutional problem. There was significant learning before formal schooling began. Then school took over the major role in learning. Now it appears that schools have forsaken learning and become part of a giant bureaucracy and employment agency.

Our superstar teachers leave the profession because they cannot earn salaries equal to their value to society. Rather, they are paid on the same scale as ineffective teachers. In most systems there is no external incentive to do an outstanding job and no consequences for unsatisfactory performance.

The lack of respect for educators among the general society also results in career changes for our brightest teachers. But the most frequent cause for leaving the profession is the inability to be in charge of the classroom. Now is the time we need dedicated teachers with an insatiable thirst for learning, to help develop the minds of our youth. We are in desperate need of role models who see learning as exciting, as fun, and as a lifelong activity. We need teachers who are expanding the PORTFOLIOS IN THEIR MINDS.

This profession needs serious change if we are to meet the challenge of preparing our children for the future. The bureaucracy must be eliminated to make it possible to focus on the major mission—the learning of our youth. Educators must be in the learning profession, not the teaching profession.

Teachers must set the direction by becoming curious learners again. The world is full of opportunity to learn and yet opportunities are overlooked and ignored. The explosion of technology and knowledge provides an incredible opportunity. How can those entrusted with creating excitement about learning not be excited themselves about learning? The very system designed to produce learners employs some educators with eyes deadened to learning. How can they inspire our most treasured resource—our children? How tragic that learning has been deserted by those society has designated responsible to create learners. True, society has changed, but if our adults were active learners they would be better able to be *Leaders of our Children.*

LEARNING AS AN ADDICTION

Learning is an activity of the mind that is expansive and addicting. Learning is a healthy addiction. There is no room for mind-altering substances to interfere with learning. Youth growing up addicted to learning do not have time to be involved in activities that deaden their eyes and eventually destroy their minds and bodies. *How do we inculcate learning into our society?*

We have to make learning a priority. We have to encourage learning to be lifelong. Each person, family, business, organization, town, and city needs to be involved. We need to apply the same planning, effort, and hype that we use for the Olympics, the Super Bowl, or other large sporting events.

Instead, when we try to improve education we form committees, commissions, and task forces to study the situation. Stop studying education and do something about learning. Give learning the same attention as a major event! Give learning the same attention as a giant concert! Give learning the same attention as sports playoffs or tournaments!

•*GIVE LEARNING ATTENTION*•

In this age of increased technology, there are more and more tools with which to learn. We must find ways to make tools, such as computers or advanced technology yet to be marketed, major components in learning. There is little time to waste.

BASIC SKILLS OF LEARNING

The basic skills of learning include thinking skills; comprehensive reading and writing skills; application of creativity; inquiry and scientific investigation; recognition and appreciation of diverse artistic expression; effective communication linkages; appreciation of other cultures set in historical context; and application of technological skills.

Skills in communication include active participation in discussion; analytical skills such as problem-solving and decision-making; expressive skills in both verbal and written forms; and group interaction skills which are so necessary in today's world. We don't need to belong to a group, but not because we don't know how to function in a group. If we are to work together in our family, workplace, and community, we must have effective group interaction skills. All these learning skills are the primary responsibility of the formal education system.

PRACTICE—PRACTICE—PRACTICE

Once we have acquired these skills, we must practice them frequently. Without practice we lose the skills we've learned. For example, you can learn to ride a bicycle, but if you want to become good at riding the bike, you must **practice—practice—practice**. You can learn to play the piano, but if you want to excel at playing the piano, you must **practice—practice—practice**.

Or you can be like me and take six years of Spanish and still not be able to speak fluently. Why? Because I didn't do the **practice—practice—practice**. This is true of any skill we learn, including playing musical instruments, dancing, cooking, playing golf, and sewing. It must be practiced to be mastered. Would it be beneficial for me to take more classes in Spanish? No, I need to practice what I already know. **Practice—practice—practice.**

•THIS IS THE KEY TO LEARNING, REFINING, AND RETAINING SKILLS•

THE CONTENT IS EXPANDING DAILY

The material available to be learned is voluminous and expanding each day. Thinking skills are used to acquire the content which includes material traditionally categorized as subjects, including literature, languages, mathematics, science, history, geography, economics, civics, art, music, physical education, and health.

When thinking skills are valued equal to content, knowledge rises to a new level—one that is useful and permanently becomes a part of the PORTFOLIO IN THE MIND. This knowledge generates excitement to learn more. Every time knowledge about a specific content is learned, the content becomes clearer and more useful. This is what creates the thirst for knowledge and activates the awesome mind. An active learner does not have enough hours in the day to discover, think, imagine, and understand the world.

HOLISTIC LEARNING

Most learning is done in total context, yet schools continue to teach as if it were compartmentalized. It is still common in classrooms to hear the familiar direction, "Now, put away your spelling books and take out your science books." However, the mind works not in a compartment but holistically. Lasting knowledge is gained when it relates to previous experiences. Children would be excited if material were taught relating to their experiences or interests.

When you watch a television show, read a book or talk to someone about a new experience, the presenters do not talk in subjects but in concepts. They don't stop to spell, then go to mathematics, then on to history. Learning takes place holistically. A short jaunt I took with a friend demonstrates this point:

We went to a casino in Connecticut. The slot machines were not operating. The tables required high minimums to play, which was uncomfortable for us. So we opted for poker. We were the only women at the table, much to the chagrin of the fishermen who were clearly annoyed that we were joining them and not the least friendly or helpful. As we both are good card players we persisted, and after losing a few hands we managed to learn the rules of the table and won several pots.

I have always enjoyed playing poker but this was my first time playing for money and it was exciting. We even became accepted at the table by these curmudgeons. However, they were glad to see us leave, as we took over two hundred dollars with us. While I learned how to play poker for money, there was also learning for all of us about judgment, love, attitude, and adapting to change.

When I returned from my short vacation, I was bursting to tell my friends about my experience playing poker. I didn't start by spelling the name of the casino and all the words associated with it. We talked about the location of the casino, the beauty of Long Island Sound and its distance from New York City and Boston, as well as its close proximity to the fishing industry and the Coast Guard Academy. We also discussed economics, *i.e.* the high estimated revenue per year; the number of machines; the anticipated growth of the casino; the addition of a hotel tower to accommodate guests.

We covered civics by discussing the impact of gambling on the community and the decision to put a referendum on the ballot to allow gambling in a neighboring city. History was discussed through the Indian tribe that settled this reservation as well as the founding fathers of Massachusetts, Connecticut, and Rhode Island. We discussed gambling and playing poker and many other topics. We talked about an experience, not a subject.

This is how people talk. This is how they learn. They do not learn in isolation by subject. We need to understand this point clearly. When we talk to someone about a particular concept, we don't talk in isolation by discipline. We need to apply a more common sense attitude to how we learn.

LEARNING ABOUT UNIQUENESS

When we explore learning by talking to others, through books, through media, and through experiences, we find that learning does not happen by subjects but rather in reference to other materials already learned.

Each person is unique. You are the only person who has had the experiences you have encountered in your life. Each of these experiences is part of your PORTFOLIO IN THE MIND. You alone use that portfolio. No two portfolios are alike. This is why siblings raised in the same environment are different. They each have encountered different experiences. They each have received different reactions from other people. They each have different talents and ideas.

•EACH PERSON HAS A DIFFERENT PORTFOLIO IN THE MIND•

Therefore, each person, when acquiring new knowledge or seeing something for the first time, puts that experience into the PORTFOLIO IN HIS OR HER MIND where it fits with a previous experience. Every judgment, value, and decision you make is based on what is already in the PORTFOLIO IN YOUR MIND. Every book you read, every person you meet is judged and stored in your portfolio based on your previous experiences. This is how we learn.

If I asked you to say good morning in Spanish and you had never heard the language, you would be unable to answer. If I said that it started with a "b," it wouldn't help. If I said the next letter was a "u," it still wouldn't help. You would have to go back and learn the basics of Spanish to be able to answer my question. We learn according to what we already have stored in the PORTFOLIO IN OUR MIND. This is illustrated in the following experience:

As I was traveling to Jacksonville, Florida, one day, I crossed a drawbridge over the St. John's River. The drawbridge was raised for what seemed a long time. There were two ambulances with sirens blaring behind me. I began to worry about being up in the air on a bridge. Since I lived eighteen years in California where I experienced major earthquakes, my previous experiences surfaced and I began to anticipate an earthquake. I probably was the only person on the bridge worried about an earthquake.

That is how people learn. That is how people develop their fears. That is how people make judgments about drawbridges.

Therefore, in our families and classrooms, each child has a different PORTFOLIO IN HIS OR HER MIND. We must learn how to expand the portfolio by **Learning to Learn.** We learn from each person we meet during the day. Each person, because of his or her uniqueness in personality and experiential background, looks at life differently. This difference and diversity is both healthy and exciting. When we view the world through these eyes, we can appreciate the differences and similarities in people — in what they eat, read, value, do for fun and what they believe.

Why then do we build prejudices about people? Why is race, religion, sex, and appearance so important? Why don't we get upset over the other differences just mentioned? We don't get mad at people who don't like classical music. Why do we dislike people because they are a different race? When you are a *Leader of Yourself*, you recognize that each person has a different PORTFOLIO IN HIS OR HER MIND. A leader can see through the different portfolios and appreciate the person. The more you learn, the more you WIDEN YOUR PERSPECTIVE. The more you learn, the more you see how difficult it is to make decisions from a limited perspective. The more you expand the PORTFOLIO IN YOUR MIND the more you learn and treasure your uniqueness.

•THE MORE YOU TREASURE YOUR UNIQUENESS,
   THE MORE YOU CAN APPRECIATE THE
   UNIQUENESS OF OTHERS•

A failure to create a society of learners is a failure to develop problem-solvers. Who will address current issues? Where will we look for the person to cure AIDS, or to solve environmental problems, or to solve problems that have not yet emerged as major issues? These issues will emerge, and then where will society be?

SO MUCH TO LEARN!

SO LITTLE TIME!

LESSONS

- Every night, recall <u>three</u> pieces of information you learned that day.

- Name at least <u>five</u> experiences, events, or pieces of knowledge you added to the PORTFOLIO IN YOUR MIND that day.

- Name at least <u>three</u> experiences, events, or pieces of knowledge you taught someone that day.

- Visit a library or bookstore and walk down the aisles. Find one section that contains information, ideas, subjects, or viewpoints about which you have limited knowledge or experience.

  > Pick up a book and browse through it.
  > Choose something out of your expertise.
  > Choose something totally different.
  > Choose something new.
  > Choose something to WIDEN YOUR PERSPECTIVE.

- Recall knowledge or new experiences learned today from a media source, *i.e.* radio, television, posters, newspapers, magazines, books, or a computer.

- Identify a CLASSROOM OF LEARNING you experienced during the day.

- Identify a CLASSROOM OF LEARNING you provided for someone else during the day.

SKILL

II

Learning to Build a Positive Attitude

FAVORABLE EQUATION— 90/10

Attitude—also known as disposition, mood, humor, temper, feeling, spirit, demeanor, poise, presence—is usually revealed by the way you present yourself to others. Although this display of attitude is easily recognized in the appearance of your body, the seed of attitude is planted in your mind and heart. This is why your attitude affects your total being.

You have learned that life is 10% what happens to you and 90% how you react. Let's look at this unbalanced equation. It is difficult and sometimes impossible to control the 10% part of that equation, but it is always possible and indeed advantageous to control the 90%. The wonderful news is that you are in control of the 90%. Take control of that 90% and make it yours.

Controlling the 90% is the answer to happiness, success, and sometimes survival, depending on the particular event in your life. You are in charge of how you feel. Outside circumstances contribute only a certain amount to your environment. You totally control your attitude. This is certainly not meant to minimize the tragedy and total disruption of your life that can occur in the 10%, but rather to emphasize your ability to gain skills to control the 90%. In a world where so much is out of your control, it is comforting to know you are in total control of your attitude.

When you put this equation in the right perspective, you become aware of your power to tackle challenges that confront you and turn them into opportunities. You have probably known a person who seems to have a full plate of challenges, tragedies, and misfortunes and yet seems to shine with a healthy, positive attitude. If you have not been fortunate to meet any of these individuals, I invite you to visit a hospital where critically and terminally ill people are receiving treatment. Or, perhaps, visit someone who has a serious disability, such as blindness or a severe physical handicap. Witness how they are able to get through the day with a smile and a good attitude despite problems and pain that might cause some people to suffer deep depression.

Too many times we become the victim of a situation. You are familiar with the responses generated by people facing tragic circumstances. They may include crying, wailing, nervous laughter, praying, or escape behavior such as running. These responses can be healthy if they are converted to action that sustains a positive attitude to endure the challenges life presents.

CHALLENGES VERSUS DAY-TO-DAY INCIDENTS

Most people dig deep and find the strength, support, and skill to face the difficult times in life. The best example of this ability is demonstrated every time there is a major catastrophe, such as an earthquake, fire, flood, tornado, hurricane, or plane crash. At this time, unknown people surface as heroes and teach important lessons in love and commitment. It is interesting that a catastrophe can be a CLASSROOM OF LEARNING. However, this CLASSROOM OF LEARNING teaches us to care, to love, and to help others. This CLASSROOM OF LEARNING teaches us to work together as a team to solve problems of great magnitude.

More common than tragic and catastrophic incidents are the ordinary day-to-day challenges. It is these daily incidents that seem to send people into a tailspin resulting in a poor attitude. Day-to-day incidents, such as

an alarm clock not going off on time,
    a flat tire,
        losing keys or glasses,
            missing a green light,
                a biting remark made by someone.

Do any of these situations sound familiar? I'm sure you can list many pages of situations and happenings that may present a challenge to you, and yet when put in the proper perspective are not really serious. If we have the skills to deal with catastrophic events, is it not reasonable to believe we can develop the skills to deal with these lesser crises? When you are the *Leader of Yourself*, you maintain a positive attitude.

RADIATE OR POLLUTE

Attitude can either radiate like the sun or pollute like a smokestack. It is one of the most contagious skills. Have you ever awakened in the morning feeling good, singing in the shower, putting on your favorite clothes, and stepping lively out the door? Then, if the first person you meet is also happy, optimistic, and cheerful, your positive attitude is raised a notch. You spread this good feeling to others. These are the people you like to meet, the people you like in your home or work environment, the people you like in your total environment. These people enhance the positive aura you radiate.

However, if the first person you meet is sad, depressed, or pessimistic, you lower your positive attitude a notch. If you meet enough of these people, you begin to feel less happy and positive. This is the contagious side of this skill and it pollutes your environment. Attitude can create a negative epidemic! Do you raise the attitude of others a notch or do you lower it? The choice is yours!

SETTING THE ENVIRONMENTAL TONE

If you do not read violent stories in the newspaper or watch television programs that start the day with sensational reporting, you will start your day on a more positive note. You cannot go out the door with visions of violence in your head and have a calm, peaceful, balanced mind, body, and spirit needed to face the days challenges.

Children cannot go to school excited about learning with visions of violence in their head. The environment is vitally important because it helps set the attitude. This skill of **Creating a Supportive Environment** will be covered later in its own chapter.

However, it is critical that you fully understand that the connections between environment and attitude are inseparable. Your attitude at home, work, and play, starting projects, or just beginning your day has a direct effect on your health, your digestion, your outward appearance, your composure, your driving, your shopping, your interaction with other people, your happiness, and ultimately your success.

In other words, the tone for the next hour, day, year, and total life is set by you. You decide your own attitude and ultimately the shape and form your life will take. This attitude is pervasive throughout your life, visible in each little detail and each little function of your day. When you are a *Leader of Yourself* you monitor your attitude constantly. No one said keeping a positive attitude is easy.

•*ANYTHING EASY HAS ALREADY BEEN DONE*•

We have many chances to monitor our attitude on a daily basis. This episode in my life gave me an opportunity to check my reaction to a comical situation.

I had an appointment at 2:00 PM and needed to stop at the post office to mail important correspondence. The temperature was 112 degrees and as usual I had many things on my mind, an armful of clothes for the cleaners, and incoming mail I had retrieved from my mailbox as well as five pieces of outgoing correspondence.

I set the incoming mail on the trunk of my car so I could unload my arms. This is not the first time I have done this same dumb thing but it had been a long time. As I was driving down one of the busiest streets in town, a gentleman in the car next to me started blowing his horn. When I lowered my window, he notified me that my mail had blown off the trunk of the car and was scattered over a block area.

I pulled over to assess the situation and decided that I needed to retrieve the mail. Drivers were blowing their horns. People were sending me unkind gestures. Body language was reaching new meanings. I drove around the block and parked on a side street, then I began the tedious task of searching for my mail, which was already dirty from being run over many times. This process took several minutes and I was now late for my appointment.

This was definitely a time for an attitude adjustment. I could stop to blame the world. However, I was the one who left the mail on the trunk of the car. I was thankful someone told me or I might have missed an important card from a dear friend, a bill, (oh, well), and even a check for work accomplished. I took three deep breaths and decided that in the total perspective of life this was only a little kink. This was no big deal!

I knew the retelling of this story would even be funny. I forced a smile and looked at the positives: a total stranger helped me by blowing his horn to notify me of my foible; I didn't cause an accident; my mail, which had blown all over the street, had ended on the sidewalk and in a dirt field instead of the road; and it certainly was a nice day instead of rainy.

I checked my attitude and decided this dumb action was not going to ruin my day. I learned from the incident to check both the hood and trunk of my car before driving away. It will probably be another few years before I do that again. What happened to me was in the 10% part of the equation—the 90% reaction part was up to me.

When I was a school principal, I had a custodian who had a negative attitude. He was a good-looking, highly competent individual who lacked self-esteem. His negativism was contagious among teachers, students, and parents. He would always meet me in the parking lot in the morning if there was something bad to report, such as graffiti, vandalism, or undelivered supplies. I could tell if there were problems by where he was when I arrived at school.

I decided to teach him skills that would result in a more positive attitude. At the end of each conversation, I would force a positive comment. Sometimes it was the sun is out today—it is indeed a nice day. Thank goodness we were in a sunny climate. That saved me many times.

He did not have a good rapport with teachers because he mostly focused on their weaknesses rather than their strengths. He would complain about the way they left their classrooms every day. So I started finding one teacher he respected and encouraged him to say something good about that person. Soon this began to spread to others.

At the end of my tenure at that school, he would come to me with complaints but always added something positive to the conversation. He always left with a positive comment. By the way, he did smile more. And, by the way, he did work better with teachers and students.

•THESE SKILLS CAN BE LEARNED•

•THESE SKILLS CAN BE PRACTICED•

•THESE SKILLS CAN BE MASTERED•

ATTITUDE IS A POWERFUL SKILL

Watch people with poor attitudes. Look at the way they dress. Look at their faces. Look at their actions. Listen to their language. Listen to the lack of laughter. See the lack of beauty. These signs of attitude are readily visible. When you observe people, you get a feeling for their attitude toward themselves, others, and the world in general.

Where do we learn the skill of building a positive attitude? Usually this skill is taught by role models who may be family members, teachers, colleagues, friends, or celebrities. Sometimes this skill is modeled by the media—by books, television, movies, newspapers, videos, or magazines. Possibly all of the above or none of the above are resources for building a positive attitude. But, because attitude is a skill:

•IT CAN BE LEARNED•

•IT CAN BE IMPROVED•

•IT CAN BE PRACTICED•

•IT CAN BE REFINED•

•IT CAN BE MASTERED•

Attitude is a mind-set. It is how you look at yourself and others. It is based on the concepts previously discussed in **Learning to Learn**. It is based on your previous experiences combined with your personality.

CONTROLLING YOUR ATTITUDE

Attitude can be changed and adapted. You are not stuck with the way your attitude is now. No matter how irritating the problem, how minor the misfortune, or how devastating the catastrophe, you alone can control your attitude.

Looking for the positives is the first step in stabilizing your attitude. This is not always easy to do but each time you use this technique it gets easier. There are many positives to be found in life's minor setbacks and even in major setbacks. We just need to learn to search for them.

The next step in controlling your attitude is to put the situation into the perspective of the bigger picture of life. Most problems will be reduced immediately in size when stacked against other problems in life.

Another technique is to take inventory of supporters who can help you fortify a positive attitude. They will assist you in learning to dig deep for extra strength to preserve your positive attitude during difficult times.

VALUE IN HAVING A POSITIVE ATTITUDE

A positive attitude helps you to be successful as a student in school; a member of a family; a worker in an organization; a member of a community; or a participant in clubs, societies, and associations. But, even more importantly, a positive attitude helps you maintain your emotional balance to survive your foibles, challenges, and even your devastations and tragedies.

It helps you live through the most sorrowful times in your life. When faced with shock, trepidation, fear, and sorrow, the answer to survival and recovery is to rebuild your mind-set. A positive attitude is the way to do this and sometimes the means to survival.

Only you , as the *Leader of Yourself*, can determine what kind of attitude you will have upon waking, rising, and living the day. Even when things are going wrong and you feel out of sorts, you alone can reverse the situation.

This positive attitude, when held by enough people, will become pervasive and permeate society. People feel better, look better, and are healthier when they have a good attitude. People work better and solve problems more effectively when they have a good attitude.

TEACHING CHILDREN TO HAVE A GOOD ATTITUDE

A good attitude does not just happen. It must be learned. It must be nurtured. It must be demonstrated by role models. It must be reinforced. Schools must teach children to build a positive attitude. Parents must teach children to have a good attitude. Adults must role model a good attitude. This is one of the most important lessons children can learn. Learning this skill provides children with a major key to survival, happiness, and success.

WORK ON THE 90%

TO

CONTROL THE 10%

LESSONS

- Occasionally monitor your attitude at home and at work for a day at least to see how you are projecting yourself.

- Check your attitude to see whether it is negative or positive when you are around certain family members, friends, colleagues, and those you see socially. Keep track to see if there is a pattern.

- When you gain confidence, ask the supporters in your life to evaluate your attitude.

- Frequently count how many times you serve as a role model for a positive attitude during a period.

- Assess where you can get help to maintain a positive attitude; identify your role models; identify your media sources.

- When you meet someone displaying a positive and healthy attitude, thank them for projecting their attitude into the world, thus helping you and each person they meet.

SKILL

III

Learning to Communicate

COMPLEXITY OF COMMUNICATION

I remember playing the telephone game at birthday parties. This game, a popular one for children, was fun but also was my earliest experience of how complex communication with others could be.

All participants sit in a circle. One child, usually the birthday child, creates a message or story and whispers it into the ear of the next child. This child then whispers what was heard into the ear of the next child and this continues until the message travels around the whole circle. The last child repeats the message, which by now is unrecognizable to the originator, who then repeats the original version. There is always a lot of laughter as to the changes in the message as the group backtracks to see who messed up the communication.

What isn't understood was that each child interpreted and filtered the message according to the experiences in the PORTFOLIO IN HIS OR HER MIND. Therefore, words, phrases, and concepts had different meanings to each child. The difficulty of communicating as demonstrated in that simple game is repeated every day in homes, schools, workplaces, and organizations. How many times have you spoken or heard these words, "That wasn't what I meant." "You're taking it out of context." "You're twisting my words." "You don't understand what I am trying to say."

Why is communication so complex? The different **forms** of communication added to the **methods** of communication and complicated by the **blocks** to communication create a tangled web in which we try to connect and relate to others.

Verbal forms of communication include—

talking,
    whispering,
        shouting,
            preaching,
                discussing,
                    lecturing.

Verbal forms of communication adding emotion include—

laughing,
    yelling,
        debating,
            gossiping,
                screaming,
                    sobbing,
                        crying.

Verbal forms of communication adding artistic talents include—

singing,
    reciting,
        acting,
            joke telling,
                story telling,
                  poetry reading.

Non-Verbal forms of communication include—

writing,
    body language,
        sign language,
            signing autographs,
                touching,
                    pointing,
                        smiling,
                            holding.

Non-Verbal forms of communication adding emotion include—

hugging,
    kissing,
        throwing things,
            pushing,
                shoving,
                    punching,
                      fighting.

Non-Verbal forms of communication adding artistic talents include—

dancing,
    composing,
        playing musical instruments,
            writing plays,
                drawing,
                    painting,
                      sculpting,
                        acting.

These examples have limitations. They do not represent every possible form of communication. Some overlap and can be listed in two if not three groups. However, the idea is what is important. There are many forms of communication. How many do you use? One form is not better than the other—just different! Different forms of communication fit different needs.

Methods of communication include—

face-to-face,
 telephone,
  fax machine,
   e-mail,
    through media,
     Internet,
      mail.

These methods of communication are certainly not all, but just examples. In fact, in this age of technology new methods are being invented even as you read this book. Some of us are still trying to learn to use the ones listed above.

BLOCKS TO EFFECTIVE COMMUNICATION

Once we have mastered the forms and methods of communicating, we can tackle the real culprit for communication problems—the blocks to communication:

Personal Filtration Systems,
 Gender Differences,
  Generation Gaps,
   Cultural Differences,
    Professional Lingo,
     Special Interest Lingo,
     Vocabulary,
      Intimidation,
      Timing.

All of us have been victims of these blocks to communication at one time. When we examine each of these blocks, it is easier to understand why communication is repeatedly identified as a major problem in relationships with family, friends, business colleagues, and society as a whole.

Personal Filtration System—As evidenced in the telephone game described earlier, your mind filters messages you receive based on past experiences and what is contained in the PORTFOLIO IN YOUR MIND. If there is no previous experience, the mind will have nothing to connect this new information to, and thus may ignore it. This is what some people refer to as going in one ear and out the other. This is one reason why children are failing in school today.

Usually we have some experience with most information received and respond according to our own perspective. It is helpful to realize that other people react the same way we do. They filter the information through their own experiences. Each person's FILTRATION SYSTEM is unique and different. This is a critical concept for teachers to understand as they work with students. It requires different instructional strategies to be used. One is not better than the other—just different!

Gender Differences—There have been volumes written about the differences in communication between men and women. Authors agree that there are significant differences between male and female communication. Women seem to take communication more personally. Men tend to be more detached. Each gender can learn from the other. However, this is not as easy as it sounds. The struggle over communication between the sexes has been an ongoing battle. The good news is that there are excellent resources to help. One is not better than the other—just different!

Generation Gaps—The differences between generations certainly are obvious in our language. The slang words as well as the current descriptors of good and bad depend on the generations. These words used to change every ten years or so to fit generational patterns. Now, however, they change more frequently. For example, what did "cool" mean to your grandparents? To your parents? To you? What does it mean to your children?

Cultural Variations—Words, phrases, idioms, and concepts have different connotations in different cultures. Not only does the language create a problem, but the contextual usage of a word or tone of voice can change from language to language. Sometimes words from one language have no exact translations into another language. This different understanding of words, phrases and concepts further increases the language barriers in a global society.

Professional—Each profession has its own set of words and acronyms. A policeman will introduce you to words and phrases like "collar," "decoy," and "packing heat," and other terminology unique to the law enforcement profession. Educators, however, are really big on acronyms, such as "SIP," which means school improvement program, or "SAC," designating school advisory council.

The computer industry is the ultimate in language not understood by a large segment of our population. This industry has introduced a whole new dictionary to communication. Words such as "bytes," "mouse," "ram," "download," "Internet," and "modems" are either new or have totally different meanings in this computer vocabulary. This sophisticated vocabulary requires serious study armed with a textbook of computer language as well as experience on a computer.

Engineers also speak their own language as do doctors and lawyers. This different vocabulary for each profession certainly creates blocks to communication.

Special Interest—Each hobby has its own lingo. Look at the "Trekies," collectors, artisans, etc. Each sport, such as basketball, football, baseball, gymnastics, ice skating, or golf, has its own lingo. For example, an eagle to a golfer is two under par on a hole; an eagle to an environmentalist is an endangered species; and an eagle to many people is a symbol of the United States. An ace to a tennis player is an unreturnable serve; an ace to a golfer is a hole in one; and an ace to a card player is a valued card.

To understand the magnitude of communication available, think about the enormous number of special interest groups, such as hobbies, sports, religious groups, etc. Let's continue.

Vocabulary—This is a topic most of us found boring in school. Perhaps it was the way it was presented. We were comfortable with our own words and those of our friends and family. A problem occurs when we all prefer to stay with our own words. By failing to increase our vocabulary to include the language used in business, professions, government, organizations and society in general, we lose many opportunities and become ineffective in our interactions with others. Your vocabulary must continue to be broadened if you are to be a *Leader of Yourself*.

You need a strong vocabulary to express yourself in speaking and writing. This need increases as changes in the world accelerate. Writing and speaking are the most vital communication skills. They are not necessarily better than other forms of expression but they are the forms most frequently used. The ability to express your needs, wants, desires, ideas, and viewpoints is essential to your success in life. This ability, directly tied to the mastery of language, gives you a key to speaking and writing.

Intimidation—One of the most common blocks to effective communication is the fear of speaking out because of feeling intimidated. People intimidate with body language and vocabulary, both forms of communication.

This intimidation is what keeps people from participating fully in relationships with family, friends, and colleagues.

As an educator I saw this intimidation demonstrated by educators toward parents, primarily in parent conferences. Granted, most of the time this intimidation is not intentional. Teachers are the most humane group of people found in a profession. They do not think of themselves as intimidators. Yet to a non-educated parent whose child is having difficulty in school, a conference with one, two, or three teachers is very intimidating.

It can create unusual defensive behavior on the part of a parent. This behavior might include non-attendance, anger, crying, yelling, or abusive language. If you add the principal, nurse or psychologist into the conference, you raise the intimidation factor significantly.

Yet educators try their best not to intimidate but to help. Their objective is to help the student perform better in school, which is best achieved by the involvement of the parent. This is a clear example of not realizing that intimidation is a block to effective communication.

Such intimidation can be partially the cause for the decline in parent participation in the upper grades. Another cause for this decline is the increase in the number of educator participants in conferences as your child climbs the grades. Interesting paradox!

Lawyers, doctors, and bankers are some professionals who may intimidate people to the point where they will not ask the necessary questions to make informed decisions that will influence their quality of life.

Timing—Another critical skill in effective communication is timing. Many children of abusive parents might escape bodily harm if they understood timing. The time to ask for money or permission to do something is definitely not in the middle of a heated domestic discussion (commonly called a fight).

To further illustrate the timing factor, look at

political campaigns. Some candidates spend thousands of dollars, yet they burn out before the election because of poor timing. In our personal life the skill of timing also plays a critical role. It can be the difference between peace and conflict; happiness and sadness; and failure and success.

There are many other blocks to effective communication. The ability to recognize and remove them is vital because communication is the number one skill needed in relationships, families, businesses, and ultimately survival in this world.

UNDERSTANDING THE COMPLEXITY OF COMMUNICATION

The first step to improving communication skills is to recognize the complexity of communication. We continually hear that communication needs to be improved. Marriage counselors often cite lack of communication as one of the major causes for the breakup of marriages. Most consultants hired to improve organizations bring forth recommendations about improving communications. When we analyze the pieces of the communication puzzle and assess our own skills, we will be on the way to becoming effective communicators. You must be an effective communicator to be *a Leader of Yourself.*

BUILDING A TOOL BAG

How do we learn skills to communicate in this complicated world? We need a large tool bag holding many different communication skills. Think of these skills as tools. The more tools you have in your tool bag, the better communicator you will be. Assess your tool bag today. What skills do you have in your tool bag and what skills do you need to add? How are you going to learn the skills you need? There are many books written on communication as well as classes designed to help you. Talk to a friend who has tools that you are missing in his or her tool bag.

The first skill for your tool bag is to understand the concept of the PERSONAL FILTRATION SYSTEM. Each person has a point of view or perspective on words, phrases, concepts and language. One FILTRATION SYSTEM is not better than another—they are just different! If you understand that the PORTFOLIO IN YOUR MIND determines your FILTRATION SYSTEM, then you can recognize that each individual has a unique FILTRATION SYSTEM. This discovery helps you understand how others receive your communication so you can determine how best to send it to make it more effective.

If you think of communication as one person trying to get an idea, thought, message, feeling, or viewpoint across to another individual, it will be easier to choose your form and method.

I learned this concept painfully as a fifth grade teacher. I had a student named Clyde who was neither physically coordinated nor popular with the other children. Clyde had no playmates at recess. The more the children wouldn't let him play, the more he pestered them.

So I decided to teach Clyde football so he could play with the other boys. I felt confident, because I am a big football fan, who watches college and professional football all weekend. It is one of my favorite pastimes. I decided that Clyde could play center. In flag football, this position did not require too many skills and would be the quickest way into the game. We practiced "snapping" the ball.

The big day came. I talked the other boys into letting Clyde play with them at recess. I told Clyde, "Just snap the ball and tackle the boy who has it." You guessed it—Clyde snapped the ball, turned, and tackled his own quarterback—one of the most popular students in the class. My plan failed because of poor communication.

It is difficult to improve communication until you figure out the other person's receiving process. This concept is a very basic tenet of effective communication that is magnified with small groups, large groups or society as a whole.

The second skill for your tool bag is learning a variety of forms and methods of communication. The more forms and methods you know, the better chance you have of getting your message across to another person. You will not use all the forms and methods but it is imperative to know they exist and be able to choose from them, just as you would choose the right tool for a project.

Some of the methods are directly linked to technology and therefore more difficult to learn. Some are becoming obsolete faster than they can be learned. Two examples of rapidly changing communication tools are the telephone and the computer.

The third skill for your tool bag is an extensive vocabulary. You can achieve this by adding to the PORTFOLIO IN YOUR MIND. As you learn through experiences, you will also increase your vocabulary — in other words, you will WIDEN YOUR PERSPECTIVE. As you increase your knowledge and interests, you will also build your reservoir of words, phrases and concepts. There are many books, puzzles, and games designed to help you build a larger vocabulary.

The fourth skill for your tool bag is timing. We all have experienced situations when we have said something, only to have it misunderstood. Sometimes it would have been better not to say anything. There are times when to say nothing is the best communication. The loudest noise of all can be silence. Yet we try to clarify and continue to shoot off our mouth. Pretty soon we have dug our hole deeper and deeper. Stop! Listen! The skill of timing is critical. You can learn this skill from the movies and television. Good comedians have perfect timing. Lucille Ball was a master of timing. Watching old *I Love Lucy* programs is a CLASSROOM OF LEARNING for timing, as well as effective use of body language.

However, a word of caution about using the media as a CLASSROOM OF LEARNING. To break into a dance in the middle of a heated discussion might not be the most effective form of communication, or maybe it would be. When you master the skill of timing, you will have that answer. People you would classify as peacemakers have excellent timing skills. They know when and how to approach difficult situations. People who excel in conflict resolution or mediation skills are masters of timing.

The fifth skill to have in your tool bag is responsibility. When you understand that you, as a piece of this large puzzle, have a responsibility to communicate, then you can overcome intimidation. Each person is responsible for communicating with others. That responsibility cannot be abdicated. When you possess effective communication skills you will no longer be concerned about anyone intimidating you.

The failure to involve all persons in the communication loop has been a major block toward full implementation of total quality management programs in the workplace. Who better to decide the most effective way to clean rooms in a hotel than housekeepers? However, many are afraid to speak out because of intimidation from supervisors. Who better to decide the education of our children than teachers? Yet many of them are afraid to speak out because they are intimidated by administrators and school board members.

This problem occurs in every business and profession. The effective workers in the trenches know how to improve productivity but they do not put forth their ideas. These people are not lazy. They are not uncaring. They are not unintelligent. They are intimidated. They lack effective communication skills. These skills can be developed, practiced, and improved. They can be mastered.

When you see your responsibility to communicate in a relationship, family, business, or organization, intimidation will stop being a block to you. You can eliminate it in your life by stepping forward and developing a large tool bag jam-packed with communication skills.

VALUE OF COMMUNICATION

The benefits of good communication include how to state facts, ask questions, formulate ideas, express opinions, make a point, challenge a viewpoint, express love, happiness, thanks, and dissatisfaction, enjoy a laugh, and compliment a person. On a broader scale the benefits include improved relationships with friends and family; a more respectful and productive work environment; less confrontation and conflict; and better problem solving.

Effective communication skills enable you to discuss issues, concerns, and problems. When conflict occurs, it can usually be traced to something someone said or didn't say—the wrong word, the wrong gesture, the wrong look. To take this problem to the extreme, people actually shoot and kill other people for saying the wrong thing or making a gesture they didn't like.

Where have we gone wrong, and how do we get back? Mastering of effective communication skills will improve you; improve your family; improve your business; improve your organizations; and ultimately improve society.

YOUR VOICE IS NEEDED—

USE IT!

LESSONS

- Assess your use of different **forms** of communication:
  Verbal,
  Verbal with emotion,
  Verbal with artistic talents,

  Non-verbal,
  Non-verbal with emotion,
  Non-verbal with artistic talents.

- Select a **form** of communication you presently don't use and practice using it.

- Assess your use of different **methods** of communication.

- Select a **method** of communication you presently don't use and learn how to use it.

- Assess your tool bag to identify the skills you possess to remove communication blocks.

- Make a plan to develop, improve, practice, refine, and master additional skills to supplement your tool bag. Your plan must include the CLASSROOM OF LEARNING you will use to accomplish this plan.

SKILL

IV

Learning to Love

LOVE IS A SKILL

Love is an emotion. Hollywood has sensationalized love in many different ways—sometimes noble, sometimes destructive. True love is never destructive but always constructive and positive. Yes, love is an emotion, but it is also a skill. Because love is a skill:

•IT CAN BE DEVELOPED•

•IT CAN BE IMPROVED•

•IT CAN BE PRACTICED•

•IT CAN BE REFINED•

•IT CAN BE MASTERED•

This is true of all skills. Playing piano, speaking foreign languages, playing football, and riding a bicycle are examples of skills that can be developed, improved, practiced, refined and mastered.

Many adults and children are born into an environment where love is not expressed freely, if at all. These children are hungry for love. Teachers see this need in the classroom with ever increasing frequency. Many years ago people learned about love from the Bible. Parents instilled love in their children. Today, love is not expressed or even discussed in some families. In fact, today love is almost missing in some families. Perhaps missing is not the correct word. Perhaps buried or dormant is a better word. It is deep in the heart. It must be brought to the surface. It must be learned. It is the only answer to combating the negativity and violence surrounding our society today. To free the love in each person, we need to teach the skill of love. It is best taught by example and role modeling.

In San Diego one day, I was in a hurry and stopped to fill a rental car with gas before returning it at the airport. I was running late as usual and had exactly 40 minutes to fill my car, drive to the airport, leave the car, take the shuttle, and catch my plane. (A side note—I arrived exactly five minutes before scheduled departure time only to have the plane be an hour late. This reinforced my bad habit of being late. When I miss my first plane I will learn to be on time.)

I paid for my gas and was attempting to open the gas tank but could not find the release to open the tank. I looked all over and was getting concerned because the time was passing.

A grubby man with long unkempt hair and scruffy clothes was watching from the sidewalk. I guess he would fit the stereotype of bum or homeless person. I asked him if he knew how to open the tank. He looked over his shoulder to see if I was talking to someone else. I repeated my question, "Can you help me open this tank?" He smiled, came over, reached in, and pulled a lever that opened the door to the tank. I thanked him and offered him five dollars for helping me. He said, "No thank you, but I would like a hug from a pretty lady like you." I looked over my shoulder to see who he was talking to. I said thank you for the compliment and gave him a hug.

By the way he was a good hugger, a very lonely good hugger. He smiled and said, "Thank you." I smiled and

said, "Thank you." We both learned a lesson in those
few minutes of our day. We both shared the wonderful
feeling of helping another person.

LOVE YOURSELF

When a person loves himself or herself, you can
see beauty in that person. Critics say love of self is egotistical but this is not so. Thinking you are better than others is egotistical. Love of self is healthy and necessary
and when spread to love of others it can change people's
lives. When you love yourself you do not talk negatively
to yourself. You do not look only for your faults but you
praise yourself for your efforts and intentions. You must
stop berating yourself. It is very damaging. Again, the
exciting realization that you control how to talk to you is
good news. You can change the messages you give yourself.

When you look in the mirror, you quickly find the
new gray hair or the weakness in your physical body. You
can reprogram yourself to notice your strong points and
embellish them. If you talked to yourself the way you
talked to your friends you would be helped. Most times
you would not treat others the way you treat yourself. You
speak negatively to yourself and often ridicule your own
actions. If you encouraged yourself the way you encourage your friends and members of your family, you would
become your own best friend. You need your own approval
more than you need the approval of others. This will let
you take giant steps toward being a *Leader of Yourself.*

How many times do you applaud or congratulate
yourself for a good deed or a job well done? How many
times do you tell yourself you are proud of you for accomplishing a difficult task? It isn't as important to tell others about your successes as it is to tell yourself.

Many times when you are in the hustle and bustle
of life, particularly when you are raising a family, you for-

get who you are and what you believe. How can you love anyone else if you don't love yourself? Can you see the domino-lessons effect? Can you see the power of mastering this skill?

About a month after my husband died, I went to the grocery store to do my shopping. As I was standing by the cashier looking blankly into my shopping cart, I suddenly realized that I didn't like anything in the cart. I had done my usual routine in the store, buying what my husband and four children liked even though I was living alone. Talk about a rut.

I stepped out of line, pulled over to the side, and began to look at each item in my basket. There were only a handful of items I truly wanted. I remember leaving the basket and walking out of the store. What was scary to me was not knowing what foods I liked but what was even scarier was that I didn't know myself. I had become a total extension of my husband and family. I had to start a search to find the real me.

LOVE HAS NO ROOM FOR ANGER

When there is love in your heart, there is no room for anger. Anger only lives in the absence of love. Anger can be the most destructive form of expression known to man. It doesn't matter whether the anger is aimed toward others or turned inward. This is an emotion which eventually turns on you, similar to a boomerang. An angry person destroys himself far more than he destroys anyone else. A *Leader of Yourself* can turn anger into a positive learning experience. While this is one of the hardest lessons to learn, it is one of the most important. The attainment of this skill brings the feeling of peace instead of the rage of anger. This does not mean that a person becomes unfeeling or stoic, but rather knows how to transform anger into true happiness by turning learning experiences into expressions of love.

•LOVE LEAVES NO ROOM FOR ANGER•

The impact of anger on a person's health and attitude is significant and sometimes can be life threatening.

TEACH NEW SKILLS

One of the ways of dealing with anger is to never expect more from someone than he or she is capable of. A very caring acquaintance who is a counselor put it this way, "Never ask a man with a broken back to run. First heal his back and then expect him to run."

If you realize that people are doing the best they can, it is easier to reduce the anger felt toward someone's actions. If you don't like the way someone is treating you, then teach him or her the skills to respond differently.

If children aren't doing their schoolwork, teach them to think, then expect them to do their assignments. If a person is yelling at you, lower your voice and role-model a different behavior—teach him to react differently in difficult situations. In other words,

*•IF YOU DON'T LIKE THE VIOLENCE AND HATRED
IN THE WORLD, TEACH LOVE•*

REPLACE THE ANGER

If you are learning from a situation, you spend time analyzing the situation rather than shouting, yelling, screaming or even fighting, all of which are actions that fuel anger. Hearts are a place for love and certainly no place for anger to hide. When anger stays in the body or mind, it grows, nurtured by evil memories that are embellished until the person is consumed.

Each person deals with anger according to his or her personality and life experience. Some people turn to rage, some to alcohol, some to drugs, and some to violence. When you are the *Leader of Yourself* you turn anger into a learning experience. You then release the hurt at the same time you grow in maturity. Learning this strategy brings a feeling of peace.

Once the unpleasant situation ends, it is critical to let it go entirely from your mind, body, and heart. Many people hold a lifetime of anger in their heart and in the PORTFOLIO IN THEIR MIND. What a tragedy for a healthy heart and what a waste of a healthy mind! With so much anger in their mind, there is no room for learning and full use of incredible talents and potential.

•LOVE IS MORE REWARDING THAN ANGER•

•LOVE IS HEALTHIER THAN ANGER•

•YOU HAVE CHOICE—CHOOSE LOVE•

PRECEPT NUMBER ONE: EACH PERSON IS DOING HIS OR HER BEST

When you rise in the morning you intend to do the best you can that day whether it be at work or play. Try hard to think about the last time you got up in the morning, went to work, or set about the tasks of the day with the main objective to do the worst possible job you could. Even when everything goes wrong you don't start out intentionally trying to have a bad day. Even when you are angry or losing control, you don't intentionally start out that way. Neither does anyone else. Events happen, things go wrong, plans go astray, all of which change the smooth course of the day. This is called life. Life is unpredictable.

For the purpose of developing this skill—love—it is helpful to realize that it is our inability to deal with the changes in our lives that causes the negativity, not the original intent of the day. Just as you don't intentionally start each day with a negative attitude, neither do others.

When you are thrust into difficult situations, remember: everyone is doing the best they can with the skills they possess. A person will perform at incredible levels when he or she knows how.

This precept forces you to look at others the same way as they look at themselves. When you practice this, you truly internalize:

•NO ONE PERSON IS BETTER THAN THE OTHER—JUST DIFFERENT!•

Each person is a teacher as well as a learner. When you teach you learn. When you provide others with skills and when you role-model understanding, love follows. Just as the number one factor in owning real estate is Location—Location—Location, the number one factor in skill development is **practice—practice—practice**. We have many opportunities to practice this concept every day in every contact we make. The practice of **precept number one** develops the skill of love.

PRECEPT NUMBER TWO: REMOVE *JUDGMENTAL SHOULD* FROM YOUR VOCABULARY

The second precept critical to mastering the skill of love is removing *judgmental should* from your vocabulary. The minute you utter a *judgmental should* you infer that you know better than the other person what is right. Most of us have our hands full living our own life. We truly have neither the right nor the expertise to make decisions for someone else. A *judgmental should* in a conversation hurts the feelings of the other person.

Judgmental should neither teaches nor creates a situation where a person learns to make choices by gathering and analyzing information. The use of the *judgmental should* with children, teens and adults will never develop thinkers or leaders. It is vital that each person learns to control his or her own life while receiving support and counsel from others.

Particularly when interacting with adolescents, the *judgmental should* is a red flag. This time of life is extremely difficult for parents even with well-adjusted and self-disciplined children. The removal of the *judgmental should* dramatically improves relationships with this delightful age group. Having experienced those traumatic teen years myself and then as mother of four children and now as grandmother of five grandchildren, I can confidently say that it makes the relationship road a lot smoother. You will feel better after you eliminate *judgmental should* from your conversations. It is difficult at first but—**practice—practice—practice** makes it easier. The removal of the *judgmental should* is a sign of respect for others. This combined with caring is a true sign of love.

APPLYING THE SKILL OF LOVE

It is impossible to feel love and hatred at the same time, or love and prejudice at the same time, or to demonstrate love and violence at the same time. In this very violent world, the only solution to ending violence is love:

•DEMONSTRATIONS OF LOVE•

•FEELINGS OF LOVE•

•EXPRESSIONS OF LOVE•

In place of the violent acts surrounding us today, we need loving actions. Don't be afraid to receive or give love. Don't be shy about love. Remember love is showing respect for and giving dignity to another.

Learn ways to express your love so that it comes from inside, blossoms, and grows for all mankind to see. I can only imagine picking up the newspaper and reading stories and articles about signs of respect, dignity, and love demonstrated. This happens spontaneously during major catastrophes or violent acts of nature, such as earthquakes, tornadoes and floods. Why can't it happen without a catastrophe?

You can only initiate love from yourself. You cannot make other people love you or their neighbor. But you certainly can do your part. You can be the *Leader of Yourself.* You must be the *Leader of Yourself.* You can fill your heart with love.

Every night, before I retire, I try to picture my heart being all pink. I try to visually remove any dark spots that may have moved onto my heart during the day. I try to see a strong heart, bursting at the seams with caring, love and sensitivity toward each person. I come in contact with the actions of my day and evaluate my thoughts and actions as they relate to love.

You cannot be responsible for other people. But you can be responsible for yourself just as I can be responsible for myself. You can be the *Leader of Yourself.* You can be responsible for your actions toward every person you meet during the day. Just think of the power emanating into the world if each person were in control of his or her interactions with others. How peaceful it would be! How many problems would begin to be solved!

It doesn't cost money to apply the skill of love. You do not need expensive gifts. A good example comes to mind when I remember an expression of love that was given to me by parents of students in a school.

One evening the school district held a beautiful reception. The chorus of students sang my favorite song, "The Greatest Love of All," which I believe has a strong message for educators. The School Board members had inscribed a plaque, with the words of the Bette Midler song "Wind Beneath My Wings," along with some memo-

rable photographs. Parents, students, staff, and community members were invited. The gifts were beautiful and I felt surrounded by love. Most gifts were engraved. The books had poignant messages written inside their covers.

One couple, who were not financially blessed, brought a gift of a small plastic bowl with a cover. It appeared empty but they insisted I remove the cover. In the bowl was a piece of paper with beautiful clear handwriting that read, "As many times as you will wash this bowl, you will never remove the love put in here for you." So little was so much!

TEACH OUR CHILDREN THE SKILL OF LOVE

Children need to be taught how to express love; how to display caring; how to participate in peace and harmony rather than media hype; and how to turn violence into love. Children can be taught by role-modeling. The following is an example of an expression of love demonstrated by junior high school students.

When I was a principal in California, one of my junior high school students was the victim of a freeway killer. It was a very violent, tragic murder. I got the call from the central office information officer identifying the victim.

The news media descended on the school like a swarm of flies and asked to accompany me as I informed the students of their classmate's tragedy. They actually wanted to interview junior high students about their feelings at this tragic time in their lives. I exploded and removed the media from the school grounds. They threatened to sue me and the words flew. They moved across the street and waited for the children to be dismissed.

After that initial challenge, my next quandary was how to tell the children. We planned a strategy in which we could lay the deceased student to rest with dignity. I spoke with each class about love, respect, and dignity. We could not do anything about the violent manner in which our student had died, but we could influence and guarantee dignity in his final memorial service. The television cameras and reporters waited across the street and began to approach the children at dismissal. The students looked straight ahead and declined to answer any questions.

At the service, we took buses of children and unloaded them at the side door, only to find the media once again sitting like vultures. The students came off the bus and one-by-one passed the cameras with dignity. With heads held high, each student declined to respond to the microphones being thrust in their faces.

They were not rude or unkind. They were showing respect and dignity for their classmate. They were displaying an expression of love. In this case, there were over 100 junior high students demonstrating that love is stronger than sensationalism. What a powerful message of love went into the community that day!

Another example of teaching children to demonstrate expressions of love involved a wonderful teacher and a tragedy in her life.

She was a popular teacher in the community, creative, innovative, caring, and loving. She was a wonderful role model — a role she took seriously. She had a boy friend whom she truly loved. They were hiking in the wilderness and had run out of food. Her friend ate a poisonous plant and died immediately. I do not want to go into the details of this tragedy because living that experience once was enough for this teacher.

However, she taught a valuable lesson that needs to be told. She returned to school shortly after the funeral. Her class was in the middle of rehearsing a play for the spring concert. She put her love for her friend into the play. The children dedicated the play to her boy friend whom they had all met and loved.

I have seen many school plays as a parent, teacher, principal, and superintendent. To this day, I have not seen a group of students perform as outstanding as those children did in an incredible performance of "Cinderella."

It was a sight to behold. Each child was superb. Each act was more spectacular than the preceding one. Everything went perfectly. The musical saw each child lift a voice in love for their teacher. They drew deep for strength. It was magic. It was an expression of love. It was teaching at its magnificent best.

There are other ways children can send strong signals of love into the community. But first the community has to send strong signals of love to its children. Do communities do this on a regular basis?

Look around and see the incredible messages of sex and violence sent to children by means of song lyrics, in movies, on television, in magazines, and daily in newspapers. Just pick up the program listings for any day on television. Jury trials, government confirmations, criminal investigations, and talk shows are examples of unsuitable CLASSROOMS OF LEARNING for children. Young children are exposed to offensive and inappropriate language continually.

I don't believe in censorship, but I do believe in smart scheduling. These programs could be scheduled during late hours when children are asleep. Many families have television operating all day. Children are very subtly brainwashed with the language of sex and violence.

How can we turn that around? We can have more educational programs during the day: programs about nature; programs where learning is fun; and biographies, in which children can see heroes and role models. These role models can be everyday people. They don't need to be superheroes or superstars.

We can have music that is uplifting, enjoyable, and educational. We can have examples of respect, dignity, and love demonstrated on television, in magazines, and in newspapers.

•WE MUST BRING RESPECT AND LOVE INTO OUR WORLD—TODAY•

Newspapers and television stations are privately owned and cannot be controlled or censored. However, they will print and televise what the public will buy and view. Change what they print and televise. It is not difficult but requires numbers of people speaking and acting together.

It will be a slow start. We can settle for a slow start. We cannot settle for no start, which is stagnancy. It is destroying our children and ultimately will destroy our society.

LOVE IS A POWERFUL SKILL!

LEARN IT!

USE IT!

LESSONS

- Look in the mirror and make a list of your assets and strengths. Do you admire others with these same qualities?

- When you arise in the morning, acknowledge that you are going to do your best that day with the skills you possess and also acknowledge that everyone else is also doing his or her best with the skills he or she possesses.

- Keep track of the number of times you use the *judgmental should* in a day. This will give you base data to know how much improvement is needed to eliminate the *judgmental should* from your vocabulary.

- At night, count the expressions of love you extended to others during the day. These might be compliments, nice gestures, favors, gifts, a smile, or a kind word.

- At night, count the expressions of love extended to you by others during the day. These might be compliments, nice gestures, favors, gifts, a smile, or a kind word.

SKILL

V

Learning to Focus Your Life

LIVE THE MOST SIGNIFICANT EVENT OF ALL—YOUR LIFE

You are born. You live. You die. The first and last events are a given. You have little control. But look at the middle event, the one in your total control—your life. Look around—this very second, this very day. This is your life. You are living it now. This is the real thing. If you don't like it, change it. Change it now! You can change it, because you are in control of your life.

DRIFTWOOD OR PERSON

It is impossible to make beneficial choices which ultimately control your life unless you focus on your goals and your purpose in life. There is a fundamental question that needs your reflection and deliberation: What are you trying to accomplish in your life? Have you spent a significant amount of time pondering this most profound question, or are you like a piece of driftwood in the ocean just drifting and bobbing along? A piece of driftwood endures some peaceful times when the sun shines brightly on a calm sea and some stormy times with turbulent seas and severe battering. A piece of driftwood has no control to change the pattern or the conditions. You are not a piece of driftwood. You are a real live being with a body, a mind, and a spirit. You have the ability and responsibility to think, make decisions, and guide your life. You cannot do any of these things if you see yourself as a piece of driftwood. Isn't it ironic that the most precious possession we have is life and we don't seem to focus and guide its progress. Time is one of your most important resources. It cannot be purchased. It cannot be slowed down. It cannot be relived.

PURPOSE IN LIFE

Set time in your day to review who you are—your gifts and talents, your strengths, your uniqueness, your journey in life. This is very important time. You were not born to just exist, but rather to be one piece of a giant puzzle called mankind. You have a purpose in life. You alone can discover what this purpose is and plan to guide your life to attain the goals that support this purpose. You can seek input, advice, and counsel, but you alone have to set your goals. You alone have the responsibility to plan the journey of your life. This path will take many turns. It will have many crossroads, some without signs or signals; it will be both uphill and downhill; and sometimes it will appear to be going in circles as if you are lost.

One time, in Washington, D.C., I was trying to find the correct highway to Reston, Virginia. I had a map and knew the road wasn't a toll road and was in the direction of Dulles Airport. But I kept taking the wrong turn, and when I crossed over the same bridge toward Arlington Cemetery I knew I was in trouble. I was going in circles literally. It was a beautiful bridge but seeing it for the third time was not helpful when I was trying to find my way to Reston, Virginia.

I started off down a different road and got lost again. This time I drove off the road and stopped at the first building, which was a church. A delightful priest in-

*side informed me I was in McLean, Virginia. He offered
me a cup of coffee because I looked so harried. I told him
about my destination and he drew me a detailed map.
We talked about being lost and how scary it can be,
and how to reverse the situation to a positive one. Then,
with my plan in hand, I tackled the formidable highway
again. Because I was much more relaxed, everything
worked out. Although I was late, the person I was meeting had been held up on her flight and was later than I.*

Maybe if you just realize that you are lost on your
path—as I did when I crossed the same bridge for the third
time—you would stop to develop a plan to find the way.
Sometimes the path is bright and sunny and sometimes
the path is dangerous, dark and stormy. The pathways of
life are not always easy but they are easier with a plan
and skills in your tool bag to accompany that journey.

LIFE FLASHES BY LIKE LIGHTNING

A very profound message was delivered by Harry
Chapin in his song, "The Cat in the Cradle." His song
demonstrates how fast life speeds along and how we fail
to identify and focus on our priorities and goals until life
has passed. This message is a wake up call especially for
parents and family members, but equally as needed for
relationships with all people.

What is the reward for accumulating material
goods, or climbing the ladder of success, if you fail to live
your life along the way? Sometimes you get so busy climbing the ladder that you forget to look underneath the ladder to see how it is secured. Your ladder may be standing
in quicksand. The next time you look down, the children
are grown, the grandchildren are grown, you receive your
invitation to join AARP, and wonder where your life went.
What happened to...? Did you have...? Life can seem to be
a series of reactions, similar to playing on the defense in
football. The way to secure the ladder is to take charge,

similar to playing on the offense in football. The way to play on the offense is to focus on your goals.

SETTING YOUR GOALS

To accomplish your dreams and desires requires taking charge by focusing all aspects of your life: your time, energy, resources, and commitment. There are certain skills needed to focus your life:

•SETTING AND PRIORITIZING GOALS—DREAMS, PLANS AND DESIRES•

•SEPARATING THEM INTO REALISTIC TARGETS•

•CHECKING ON YOUR PROGRESS•

These skills will lead you toward realization of your goals. Any successful business operates on a plan that includes its mission, goals, objectives, and bottom-line results. Isn't your life more valuable than any business? In a personal life the mission equals purpose in life; the goals equal dreams and desires; the objectives equal targets; the bottom-line results equal quality of life. Decide what you want to do and then put your resources and energies toward accomplishing that goal.

TIME FRAME FOR SETTING GOALS

At least once a year, schedule time to set goals. This is most easily accomplished by choosing a day that you will remember. Choose a special day, a day in which you have time to reflect and focus on you and your life. Many people select New Year's Day. However, your birthday, or any other day that is a milestone to you, is equally appropriate. Staying with the same day each year helps make setting goals an annual part of your life. Choose a day that will be easy to remember in order to make annual goal setting a routine in your life.

Do not confuse goal setting with New Year's resolutions which are usually about self-improvement, unrealistic, and many times tongue-in-cheek. Effective goal setting is a meaningful exercise and an energizing substitute for New Year's resolutions. A time equally as valuable is your birthday, when you are reminded you are one year older and life is moving along.

EXAMPLES OF GOALS

Goals can be material, such as acquiring a new car, a new home, new furniture, or more money. Goals can be health-oriented, such as becoming physically fit, stopping smoking, reducing drinking, losing weight, getting a checkup, or adjusting to a disability. Goals can be personal, such as meeting a mate, having a baby, getting a job, taking a vacation, completing school, finding or advancing in a career, or using artistic talents for expression. Goals can be profound, such as becoming a successful person, being a supportive, loving parent, having healthy supportive relationships, becoming a lifelong learner, or finding your purpose in life.

SETTING REALISTIC GOALS

Goals must be realistic and attainable. If goals are set too high you may get discouraged, tired, and find them difficult to reach. When you don't reach your goals you begin the anger cycle, which includes negative talk to yourself. You turn this anger inward, which can cause damage to your self-esteem, illness, or depression.

This happens when you see yourself as a failure. You are not a failure. You just set your goals too high. Set goals realistically to improve your self-esteem and ultimately your health.

If you want to start walking or running, don't aim for several times a week. Aim for once a week. If you walk twice a week, you will be proud of yourself. When you are proud of yourself, you build your self-esteem and grow stronger emotionally. You give yourself a big boost in your own eyes.

As you build your confidence after achieving many boosts, you will raise the bar in your goals and targets. Only when your self-concept is healthy and positive does your attitude become pleasant and positive. As your confidence builds, your self-concept gets stronger, your attitude becomes positive, and you grow strong emotionally. Being strong emotionally is critical to being a *Leader of Yourself*. When you are a *Leader of Yourself* all things are possible.

PRIORITIZING YOUR NEEDS

Before you can set goals, you first need to prioritize your needs to really know what you want. As you grow older you find your choices lock you into particular habits, lifestyles, dreams and desires. It is very difficult to change your course or career path once it is set. It is difficult but not impossible. It certainly takes skills which have been refined and mastered to make this change.

I always introduce myself as born married with four children. My choices on graduating from high school were to go to college to be a teacher; to complete nursing training as did my mother and sister; to go to secretarial school; or become a housewife. I realize this is an overgeneralization of my generation, but it was fairly accurate, particularly if you lived in a small town. Times have certainly changed for women.

When you go to school to prepare for a certain job or career, often times you lock yourself into it. Other careers become difficult to imagine. Because you are more familiar with those jobs or careers in which your family or friends are engaged, you rarely look outside the known to find a job that is interesting, exciting, and a match for your talents and interests. It is difficult to believe your security is not found in a company, profession, or organization but rather in your knowledge, your talents, your attitude. Your security in life is you!

CHANGING YOUR GOALS

You must be prepared to change your goals when the need occurs. That need can come with an important or major event in your life: an event such as marriage, birth of a child, death, divorce, sickness, a natural catastrophe, etc. Many times these events interfere with attaining goals, and yet we fail to adapt or modify but rather travel down our path without setting goals at all. At least if we set goals once a year we will not be like driftwood for more than one year but will get back on track as soon as possible.

When my husband died after 30 years of marriage, a close friend suggested that I needed to have some fun in my life. She asked me, "What is fun to you?" "What are your interests?" I didn't know. My fun and interests had been based on the interests of my husband and children. My life had centered around the children, my husband, and work. I could not describe what fun was for me. It took months of thinking, a lot of painful reflection, and a lot of reading to begin to understand what I thought was fun and what interested me.

This scenario is played out many times in the lives of mothers when their children leave the nest. Yet this activity—having fun—is something people take for granted. How can you set goals to have fun, which is an appropriate goal for someone trying to get on with a new life, when you don't know what fun is? Don't get ahead in your planning and forget to ask and confront the difficult questions.

SETTING REALISTIC TARGETS

Once you have goals clearly defined in your mind, the next step is to break them into realistic targets set for regular intervals. Depending on your skills in this area, choose the most meaningful time frame for you. If you are new at setting goals and targets or feel as if you lack direction, probably setting a daily target will be most beneficial as you begin. Once you feel more focused, you can move to weekly targets and then to monthly targets. Do not feel badly if you stay on daily targets for a period of time, because this is just helping you to focus your life.

Remember each person operates at his or her own pace and in his or her own comfort zone. This pace is different from anyone else's pace and varies with the person and circumstances. There is no standard or model to use for comparison. Each person is on a different time line. The goal of this book is to help you inch along your pathway. This goal does not include comparing yourself to any other person.

A *Leader of Yourself* spends time developing and refining targets until they become habit or at least an integral part of daily life. The only way to accomplish goals is to make them an integral part of your life. Try writing them on cards that you keep in your wallet or on a dresser. Keep them some place where you see them daily.

I set goals once a year, usually on New Year's Day just before the college football bowl games. I try to set five goals: one personal, one professional, one learning, one family, and one health and fitness. Every month I make a list of targets designed to accomplish these goals.

Every day, I try to work something into my schedule toward fulfillment of one goal.

For example, in the family area, a yearly goal might be to keep in close communication with my four children and five grandchildren, who live in different states.

Monthly targets include watching for good airfares to schedule visits to them or for them to visit me; listing the birthdays that need cards and presents; visiting a card store occasionally to select cards that will provide a happy moment or make them smile; clipping an item or a cartoon from the paper that they may find humorous.

Weekly targets include calling each child or my mother by telephone and e-mailing each child and grandchild.

My children are very close to me and very close to each other because I make that a goal. The support, caring, and love that comes from this kind of relationship is priceless, cannot be bought, and is extraordinary. Miles do not divide families. It is communication, caring, and thought that nurture the closeness of a family.

This plan requires a written goal along with targets that are acted upon methodically, or good intentions may get lost in the busy day-to-day activities. Your family deserves good intentions turned into actions. It doesn't take long when you plan and when you are goal-oriented. Targets that are set daily, weekly, monthly or quarterly are designed to insure that you are consciously focusing on your goals. You must not focus on the future so much that you forget to live your life today. You must not become the victim of a life that slipped by.

EVALUATING PROGRESS

Accomplishments guide you toward success. That road to success must be evaluated regularly, based on specific criteria. This evaluation lets you know how you are doing. It doesn't take a lot of time, but it is an integral part of the success or failure of attaining your goals and ultimately the success or failure of your life. Think of it as fine tuning or a reality check. Think of this evaluation as resetting your goals and targets rather than as failing.

A *Leader of Yourself* evaluates life through everyday actions. This evaluation includes time for thinking and reflection, time for a balanced life. Are your goals balanced in five areas or are they concentrated in one part of your life? Are your goals continually focused on one part of your life? A balance in your life is vital to being the *Leader of Yourself.* It is okay to be off balance occasionally. There are times when one part of your life needs more focus than another. But if this imbalance persists, reassess your goals and targets.

The most difficult challenge for people driven by a career is to find time to evaluate and reevaluate goals. They fail to schedule—

•TIME TO RELAX•

•TIME TO REFLECT ON PERSONAL GOALS•

•TIME TO ENJOY SURROUNDINGS•

The inner peace that comes with this reflection is possible in each person who shares the earth. Once you experience the inner peace of being on track with your life, you will become unwilling to relinquish that time again.

But most importantly, once you learn to focus your life by setting goals and targets and monitoring your progress, you become in control of yourself, making you a *Leader of Yourself.* When you are *a Leader of Yourself* your life has more meaning and you can experience true happiness and success. Anything becomes possible once you have a plan for focusing your life and allocating your most important asset—time.

FOCUS YOUR LIFE—

TIME IS PRECIOUS!

LESSONS

- Select a day in the year that will be your refocusing day. It can be your birthday, New Year's Day, or any other day that has a significant meaning to you.

- Develop goals that will be your major emphasis this year. There is no magical number. If you are new to goal-setting, start with one goal. If you are experienced, choose five goals. Try to make these goals in different categories, such as personal, family, professional, or health.

- Prioritize your goals according to the need and circumstances surrounding you at this time.

- Define realistic targets for each goal on a daily, weekly, or monthly schedule.

- Schedule your activities into your personal calendar.

SKILL

VI

Learning to Use Personal Power

PERSONAL POWER IS A GUARANTEED RIGHT

You have constitutional rights. You have civil rights. There are laws and volumes of court transcripts ensuring your legal rights. However, your most precious and indisputable right is to control your mind. The control of your mind is personal power. Your most basic right is the right to think for yourself. To think for yourself is control of your mind. Control means power.

•TO NOT UNDERSTAND POWER IS TO NOT HAVE ANY•

This right is guaranteed by birth. You must not give this power over your mind to someone or something else, but rather you must strengthen your control over your own mind. Learn to use your mind. Learn to use personal power.

•PERSONAL POWER = CONTROL OF YOUR MIND•

Power is usually depicted as being used by bullies or people during a show of force. Yet the strongest power is the power of the mind. The use of that power is personal power. Power over your mind simply means that you alone determine your thoughts, actions, values, and judgments.

Power means to control. When you look at personal power it means to control one's own person. This concept is not widely discussed because people tend to connect power with evil or manipulation. On the contrary, the use of personal power by each individual is extremely positive. When you use personal power you are preventing yourself from being a victim. This does not mean you do not seek advice or counsel. It does not mean you do not gather information, analyze, and take the necessary steps to make decisions. But it does mean that you alone are the person who decides what you will do.

POWER OF YOUR MIND

Personal power means you are in charge of your own mind. That seems simple enough; however, it obviously is not simple when you realize how many people are not in control of their own mind, thoughts, and life. Extend this to their own beliefs, values, judgments, decisions, and ideas. How many people that you know have either given away their power to others or to various forms of addiction? Either way, they are not in control of their mind.

It is easy to give away your personal power: You can give your power to friends, family, parents, spouse, or to addictions such as alcohol, drugs, overeating, bad habits, or other forms of obsession. Anything that takes up an inordinate amount of thinking time takes power from you.

When YOU choose to think about someone or something you are in control of your own thoughts. When you think about someone or something else all the time, you have given away your power to that person or thing. When this happens, that person or thing is controlling your thoughts. The same is true of any form of addiction or obsession. It is dangerous or risky to allow someone or something to have power over your thoughts. That is power over your mind. It is a violation of you, the most serious violation you will have in your lifetime. This is the most serious rape of all—the rape of your mind.

•IS SOMEONE OR SOMETHING ELSE IN CONTROL OF YOUR MIND?•

•IS SOMEONE OR SOMETHING ELSE DECIDING YOUR THOUGHTS?•

For example: When you and a friend have a dispute, a disagreement, or a fight, your mind focuses on that person totally. You end up in constant turmoil thinking about the other person: about the hurt from the other person; about how you can get even, and all sorts of negative thoughts. If your thoughts are wishing ill will to someone, then you have really given your personal power to a situation.

Consider how much time you spend thinking about people you dislike or with whom you disagree. If you become scared or frightened, you begin to have negative thoughts. When this happens, you have given your power away to someone or something else. What a waste of time! Assert power over your mind and reclaim your thoughts.

•TIME IS ONE OF YOUR MOST IMPORTANT RESOURCES•

•TIME CANNOT BE PURCHASED•

•TIME CANNOT BE SLOWED DOWN•

•TIME CANNOT BE RELIVED•

RECLAIMING YOUR POWER

The first step to reclaiming your power is to determine to whom or what you have given it. Keep track of whom and what you think about during the day. For example, have you ever sat in church or a theater and not had your mind there? When you bring your body to a CLASSROOM OF LEARNING, you must also bring your mind. Many times your mind may appear to be separate from your body.

A certain amount of daydreaming is healthy when done intentionally. Everyone needs some whimsy and dreaming in life. This is critical to well-being. However, there are times when it will interfere with relationships, family, work, and learning.

You cannot WIDEN YOUR PERSPECTIVES or add to the PORTFOLIO IN YOUR MIND unless you are in control of your mind. As I work with teachers in professional development, I always remind them that they can get the <u>body</u> of the student there, but the real challenge is to get the <u>mind</u> of the student into the CLASSROOM OF LEARNING. This goes back to a basic understanding of the mind. Many school dropouts are present in class every day!

CHANGING THE CHANNEL

A second way to reclaim your personal power, when you are thinking about someone or something else obsessively or negatively, is to CHANGE THE CHANNEL. When you are watching television and you don't want to watch a certain program, you use the remote control to CHANGE THE CHANNEL. When you want different music on the radio you change the station. Think of your mind as having many channels which can be changed by a remote control. Unlike the television remote control, you totally control the remote control for your mind.

CHANGE THE CHANNEL to a channel of your design. Design several different channels for yourself.

My favorite channel change picture is a beautiful beach with sparkling white sand, surrounded by tall palm trees and gorgeous fragrant flowers including orchids. My beach resembles a beach in a remote part of Hawaii. The sun is shining brightly and there are wispy white clouds floating against the blue sky. The waves are gently flowing to the shore. This scene is refreshing and tranquil.

When someone else is controlling time in my thoughts, I CHANGE THE CHANNEL and slide in my picture. This allows me to think of something I find very relaxing and peaceful which allows me to get control of my mind. Being able to CHANGE THE CHANNEL helps if you are preoccupied with negative thoughts, scared, or facing difficult challenges in your life. This technique is valuable and even essential at times of stress or when faced with tragedy.

One time, when my children were young, we had been out running errands. As we approached a dangerous intersection near our house, there were two little boys, ages five and three, crossing the street by dodging cars. This intersection had no traffic light or stop sign although the community had been trying to get one installed. A man was warning them to stay on the sidewalk and out of the street.

I took my children home and about ten minutes later returned to the corner store for milk. As I approached the intersection, I saw a crowd of people crying. Looking into the street I saw the bodies of the children. They looked like rag dolls. They had been hit by a truck whose driver had not seen them. I thanked God that my children had not been with me to see this traumatic picture.

For many weeks those bodies appeared in my mind. Finally, I CHANGED THE CHANNEL. I put a new design in my mind. It helped tremendously.

Learn how to CHANGE THE CHANNEL. It works to help you gain control of your thoughts. CHANGING THE CHANNEL can also help at night. When you go to bed, put a peaceful picture in your mind. It helps with your stress. It helps you sleep better. Design different programs for your channels. Think of them as old-fashioned test patterns for the mind. This skill has pulled me through heavy tragedies and is a powerful technique to help you gain control of your thoughts.

BUILDING A SUPPORT GROUP

A third way to reclaim your power is to build a support base of individuals you trust. This support can either be on a one-to one or a small group of people who share a common problem. There is a big difference between getting help and encouragement, and letting others make your decisions. There are many people who can support you, but you need to identify them before you need the assistance.

You may choose religious leaders, a spouse, parents, relatives, friends, teachers, counselors or others. Intentionally seeking advice on how to reclaim your power is not giving up your rights. In fact, knowing when to ask for help and support and how to use it is a valuable skill.

POWER INCLUDES RESPONSIBILITY

The discussion of power must also include a discussion of responsibility. Responsibility for self is critical. At times when you are angry, hurt, tired or disappointed, it is easy to blame others for the problems in your life. It is easy to let others be your leader. When you allow someone else to be in charge of your decisions, you give away your power. This is devastating and futile, because you can never give away the responsibility. You can never give away responsibility for yourself to someone else. You may try, but it doesn't work. It will always return to you. The responsibility for controlling you belongs entirely to you.

MAKING YOUR OWN DECISIONS

Therefore, if you cannot give away the responsibility, why would you give away the power? You must keep this power within yourself because you know what is best for you. If you feel that others know what is best for you, then you have already given away that power. This is the time to get it back. You can only retrieve it when you learn skills to help you.

Why do people give their power to others? Sometimes it is because if the decisions fail—they will not feel responsible. Have you ever seen something go wrong and everyone look for someone to blame? Some people take comfort in blaming others. You can also blame someone else when things go wrong if you didn't contribute to the decision. It is not necessary to feel comfortable. It is necessary to be responsible.

This abdication of your responsibility is many times viewed as safer and easier. It is not easier and certainly is not safer, because you are ultimately responsible for your decisions and choices, no matter who makes them. Isn't it better to control them by making them yourself? Not to do this is false security as well as mind control by others. This can be very dangerous behavior. Power is not to be taken lightly. It is vital to possess your own power, and equally important that no one else exerts power over your mind.

MASTERING PERSONAL POWER ELIMINATES ADDICTIONS AND OBSESSIONS

Let's talk about addictions and obsessions—those things in life which you allow to have power over you. They can be smoking, gambling, exercise, sports, puzzles, drugs, food, alcohol, even soft drinks. Anything you cannot exist without having or doing is an addiction. Anything done to the extreme is an obsession. Be wary of both! Give close scrutiny to your activities and habits. Do you control them or do they control you? There is a big difference. One is choice; the other is control. Identify those activities and habits that you perceive are controlling you, and begin to reclaim your power. When you do this, you will eliminate these addictions from your life. Will this be easy? Absolutely not. But until you identify where your power is you cannot develop a plan to reclaim it.

•REMEMBER: ANYTHING EASY HAS ALREADY BEEN DONE!•

VALUE OF PERSONAL POWER

When you have reclaimed your personal power—the control of your mind—you become a *Leader of Yourself*. As the *Leader of Yourself* you become influential in your environment. You enhance your family, community, workplace, and organizations. You participate in discussions, group decisions, and problem solving. You seek out CLASSROOMS OF LEARNING to WIDEN YOUR PERSPECTIVES and add to the PORTFOLIOS IN YOUR MIND.

Your participation, viewpoints, and ideas are valuable. You are like one piece in a giant puzzle, which has billions of pieces. Each piece is essential to the puzzle. Each piece has a responsibility to the completion of the puzzle. One piece is not better than the other—just different! The world will only function effectively as a peaceful place that overcomes problems, concerns and challenges when each piece fits into the puzzle.

This is what society needs: the viewpoints of each

person, the ideas of each person. Each person is important to the total world, not only to himself or herself. Each person has a contribution to make. Start making your contribution by realizing and using your personal power.

PERSONAL POWER IS YOURS TO POSSESS!

USE IT WISELY!

LESSONS

- Make a list of the people to whom you have given your power. The first place to begin in reclaiming power is to locate where you placed it.

- Identify which activity, hobby, habit, or addiction is controlling your thoughts and time.

- Prepare a plan to reclaim the power from the people you identified as having it.

- Prepare a plan to reclaim the power from the activities, hobbies, habits, or addictions you identified as having it.

- Design several pictures you can use to CHANGE THE CHANNEL in your mind to help reclaim your power.

- Identify those individuals who can provide support for you as you reclaim your power.

SKILL

VII

Learning to Create a Supportive Environment

VALUE OF A SUPPORTIVE ENVIRONMENT

"Supportive environment" sounds like a trite, over-used sixties phrase. However, mastery of this skill provides the outside structure that enables you to learn the other nine skills. It is this supportive environment that paves the way and makes it easier to learn, to have a positive attitude, to love, to use your personal power in a positive way, to communicate, to set and achieve your goals, to adapt to the changing world, to grow from the challenges life presents, and to embrace a commitment.

PHYSICAL HOME ENVIRONMENT

A *Leader of Yourself* knows how to create and maintain a supportive environment in which to live. This starts with the physical home environment. The task is to create surroundings that are comfortable and positive; surroundings that are peaceful. This environment may be different at various times in your life. It also probably will change at a faster pace now than in years past.

In the 1920's, for example, people were born in one

town, lived in one town, and died in the same town. Today that scenario is very different as people move frequently. Change in location can diminish the support of the extended family as well as create a feeling of isolation and alienation from networks of social and professional friends. This in turn causes a need to create a different form of extended family and networks, and will be addressed later in another skill, **Learning to Adapt to Change**.

EARLY YEARS

As a child or teenager, creating a supportive environment may take the form of hanging posters in your room, or painting the room your favorite color. If you share a room, it may mean decorating your little corner, arranging your half of the dresser, or putting favorite things on your bed. Some children enhance their environment with backyard tents or large doll houses, while some choose tree houses or secret places away from the house.

The beauty or the expense of the environment is not the issue—what is important is your ability to make it comfortable and to create your own little corner of the world.

When I was a child growing up in Brooklyn, New York, I lived in a large, 64-unit apartment house. We didn't have a yard. We had a cement strip about 12 feet wide that ran behind the house (in retrospect it was ugly), and we had the roof, which we lovingly referred to as Tar Beach. It was actually tar and hot in the summer but it was safe, private, and comfortable. At night you could see the fireworks from Coney Island. They were beautiful.

These two locations were our yard and we used blankets and cushions to make them comfortable. We sat on either cement or tar but we fixed them up so they were great places to play.

Meanwhile, one of my friends who lived in a brownstone had a beautiful large doll house you could walk into, and her brother had a tree house. They actually had a yard, with a patio. Ours was just as great. We used imagination and a lot of creativity. They were both supportive environments. Neither setting was better — they were just different!

ADULT YEARS

Creating a supportive environment can be a challenge when raising a large family. Sometimes the noise level can rise to new heights, particularly when there are teenagers in the family. However, the most comfortable and peaceful environment may also be one that includes children. The innocence of children, their enthusiasm, curiosity, and laughter, their silliness and giggling all produce comfortable environments.

Pets many times can contribute to a comfortable environment. Even though they are a lot of work, they add to the joy of a home. At one memorable time in my life, our home included me, my husband, four children, two dogs, a cat, a hamster, a rat, two mice, a snake, an aquarium, a rabbit, and a guinea pig. All that was missing was a sign that said ZOO.

A house does not need to be luxurious or roomy. It needs to be comfortable, and reflect the personalities of those who reside there. It needs to be a home.

I had a very happy home in a plain, cold apartment in Brooklyn, New York. It was cold because the apartment was rent controlled and the landlord was trying to freeze us out because he could not raise the rents. He wanted everyone to move so he could charge more to new tenants.

His scheme didn't work because the people got along well and lived together in a harmonious way, Catholics, Jews, and Protestants — Irish, English, German, Polish, and French — all sharing a close space in the heart of the city. This home was comfortable because there was peace, laughter, and love.

There was little money for food, no money for frills. We had to walk up four flights of stairs to get to our apartment. The furnace in the basement kept catching on fire in the winter and we would have to run down those same four flights of stairs and exit right past the oil furnace which was usually in danger of exploding.

We had to take our bikes down four flights of stairs to ride them. We had no grass or lawn. Still, our home was comfortable because it had our favorite couch, our favorite chair, our favorite radio and phonograph. We played our favorite music and read our favorite books from the library. We baked our favorite cookies. We decorated during the holidays with our favorite decorations. We spent a lot of time in our comfortable church. There was peace and love.

I have lived in many beautiful homes since then, even one featured in "Better Homes and Gardens" for the best design in the mountains. None was more comfortable than that simple, cold apartment. There was peace. There was love. There was a supportive environment.

OUR ENVIRONMENT CHANGES

As you move to new cities and towns, sometimes you long for the environments of your past, but what you really want is the supportive environment of the past. This can be created. You do not have to wallow in the sorrow of missing the past. You can create a supportive environment by changing your environment as your needs change. You just have to understand clearly what you are doing. You need to understand you are CREATING A SUPPORTIVE ENVIRONMENT. That environment can have a different structure; it can have different furnishings; it can have different colors; it can be in a different location; or it can have different people in it. None of these factors are barriers to CREATING A SUPPORTIVE ENVIRONMENT.

•ONE ENVIRONMENT IS NOT BETTER THAN THE OTHER—THEY ARE JUST DIFFERENT•

Many times as members of the family grow and leave the nest and possibly move away, we miss a part of them. We miss our old environment. The problem arises when we keep the same environment with some of the cast of characters missing.

A more supportive environment might be created from a new environment—a blending of the old and new. Maybe keeping cherished mementos. Choose what is supportive for you. You must understand that only you know what is supportive and comfortable.

HOME ENVIRONMENT

We underestimate our physical environment and the impact it has on attitude, personality, and total being. Yet this is an easy place to demonstrate leadership. Examine your environment from a new perspective—one of supporting your attitude and your total being. Make it comfortable. Who else will do this for you? Who else knows what makes you comfortable? Who else knows what makes you peaceful?

You are the *Leader of Yourself.* You must take charge of your own physical environment, which includes furniture, colors, curtains, carpets, and much more: photographs, pictures, statues, music, television, books, magazines, newspapers, and anything else that influences your attitude and how you feel when you are in that home.

I love flowers, candles, books, music, and soft colors. These must be in my environment. I may not have groceries in my refrigerator because I have been too busy to get them or been out of town. But I must have live flowers. I will go to a supermarket in the middle of the night to buy flowers for my home. I have been known to go out in a storm to buy a book or a candle. I have determined they are important ingredients in supporting my environment.

CREATING A SUPPORTIVE HOME ENVIRONMENT

The first step to building a supportive home environment is to identify what is important to you. You can do that by deciding what would cause you to go out in a storm. What do you like? What makes you comfortable? What makes you happy? Everyone is different. What is in the PORTFOLIO IN YOUR MIND about a pleasing and nurturing home? Dig deep and find out. Think about yourself and what makes you feel good. You've heard the phrase, "Take time to smell the roses." For some it isn't roses, it's herbs. You can't take time to enjoy what makes you feel good if you can't identify what it is.

WORK ENVIRONMENT

Another critical environment is where you work. Because you spend many hours at work, it is critical that it be a supportive environment. If each person were in a good work environment, each organization would be more productive. People work best when they are in a job where they feel supported. An organization in which employees feel good about themselves is more successful and has higher productivity. It is critical that you choose your work environments. When enough people choose their environment, work productivity in our society will increase.

Many times we feel chained to a bad environment. We feel trapped in a work situation. There is always a way out of any situation. Sometimes it takes longer than other times to get out of a bad work environment. You just have to be a *Leader of Yourself* and make the decision about where you want to work.

You can tell to what degree you like your job if you

can answer the question, "Would you do this work for no pay?" If you are not satisfied where you work, then you need to put a plan in place to make a change. It may take time but it will happen and you will feel better knowing you are the *Leader of Yourself.*

CREATING A SUPPORTIVE WORK ENVIRONMENT

You may have to do without some pleasures of life for a period of time. You may have to struggle, you may have to go to school for additional training. These are all your choices. A *Leader of Yourself—*

•KNOWS THERE ARE MANY CHOICES AND EXAMINES THE POSSIBLE CONSEQUENCES OF EACH CHOICE•

•PREFERS TO MAKE THE CHOICE RATHER THAN REMAIN IN AN UNSUPPORTIVE ENVI-RONMENT•

•BELIEVES THAT SECURITY LIES IN SKILLS, COMPETENCE, AND CONFI-DENCE•

The way to increase that security is to become more skilled, increase confidence, and become a lifelong learner. As you broaden the CLASSROOMS OF LEARNING, and add to the PORTFOLIO IN YOUR MIND, you increase your opportunities for work and your ability to make better choices. As you make better choices in your work environment, you increase your job security exponentially.

RELATIONSHIPS ENVIRONMENT

The next important environment is that of rela-tionships. This is where we may limit our thinking to

intimate relationships rather than broadening our view to include relationships with every person we meet. You have daily relationships with people:
where you live,
      on your way to and from work,
          where you work,
              where you shop,
                  where you play.

You have ongoing relationships with friends, associates, members of your family, church, clubs, and athletic teams. These relationships have different purposes and intensities. Some relationships are very short term while others are long term. Some relationships are one-time meetings while others last an entire lifetime. The skill to interact effectively in all different kinds of relationships is critical to being a *Leader of Yourself*.

If you allow others to control your relationships, you experience anger, hurt, disappointment, isolation, resentment, rejection or frustration. You have experienced these negative feelings at one time or another. The skill to control these feelings lies within you. Therefore, if you want to experience friendliness, humor, happiness, love, kindness, caring, support, joy and other positive feelings, you must take a risk as the *Leader of Yourself*. This is not easy, especially for those who have lacked skills in interacting with people for a long time.

As a *Leader of Yourself*, you develop skills to support your relationship environment. You may stumble along the way, but each time you will refine your skills by **practice—practice—practice** until you encounter each relationship with excitement and a positive feeling as you learn.

CREATING A SUPPORTIVE ENVIRONMENT FOR RE-LATIONSHIPS

What skills are needed to create a supportive environment for relationships? You start by assessing each situation to see how you feel. If you feel good, happy, excited, caring, or other positive feelings when you finish talking with someone, that is a good relationship. If you feel sad, depressed, angry, frustrated, or other negative feelings, and it happens each time you talk to the same individual, that is a relationship that needs to be examined. It is definitely questionable and may be a relationship that needs to be ended.

Analyze each situation until you know why you feel positive or negative. You can start by asking basic questions about the other person or persons. Have you ever gone out with a group and really felt out of place? You probably should question why you went with that group. Find people with whom you are comfortable and whose company you enjoy. When you stop seeing people who make you feel bad or negative, you will begin to realize that you feel better. If they are important in your life, help change their behavior when they are around you.

For example, I have never enjoyed off-color jokes. I have openly expressed that feeling. Therefore, people simply do not tell that kind of joke or story around me. They have plenty of opportunity to share those stories with friends who really enjoy them. This makes me feel better and creates a supportive environment for me.

If you don't like to be where people are drinking, don't sit in a bar. If you don't like to be around smoke, don't sit where people are smoking. If you don't like loud and crude behavior, don't stay when that behavior begins. In other words, pay more attention to your surroundings and choose your environment so that it reflects what is supportive for you. This also helps others to learn what you enjoy. This does not mean stomping out of a group, berating a group, or preaching to a group, in a missionary way. This means choosing your own supportive environment, choosing your own surroundings. This means being a *Leader of Yourself*.

ENJOY THE BEAUTY

Beauty is an important part of your life, whether it is the beauty of people, animals, flowers, buildings, music, art, or just seeing the beauty in nature, such as a sunset or a body of water. Too many times, while caught in the fury of life, the beauty of life escapes our thoughts.

•A LEADER OF YOURSELF NOTICES AND ENJOYS THE BEAUTY SURROUNDING HIM OR HER•

•A LEADER OF YOURSELF HAS LEARNED TO REPLENISH ENERGY AND GOOD FEELINGS FROM THIS BEAUTY•

How many roses have you smelled lately? How many times have you seen and appreciated the beauty that surrounds you? Do you have to look really hard to find beauty in your environment? Then change your environment.

One day I was working in downtown Los Angeles in a community of old dilapidated homes with security bars, graffiti, trash, beer cans, and empty liquor bottles lying around dirty streets and sidewalks.

In the middle of this decaying neighborhood was a little rundown house with a beautiful rose bush in the front yard. On the bush were three beautiful roses as if a symbol of hope and what could be for this community. Two senior citizens were enjoying them. I wondered how many children or young people noticed them on their daily trek to school.

Right in the middle of this frightful disaster area was a sign of what could be. Build your environment around what can be, build your environment around symbols of hope and your whole being changes.

CREATE AND ENJOY THE

BEAUTY IN YOUR

ENVIRONMENT!

LESSONS

- Look at the immediate environment of your home.
  Make a list of low-cost items that would improve
  it. Develop a realistic time line to add these items
  to your environment.

- Make a list of items you can remove from your
  environment to make it more supportive. Make a
  realistic time line for removal of these items.

- Look at your work environment. Look closely and
  objectively at your job assignment and your satis-
  faction with that assignment. Decide if this is a
  supportive environment for you. Ask these questions:
  Is this work utilizing your talents?
  Is this work interesting to you?
  Would you volunteer to do this work?
  Is there a different line of work in which you
  would rather be engaged?
  What skills would it take to be employed in a
  line of work that interests you?

- Consider the people you meet on a daily basis.
  List those who make you feel good when <u>you</u> leave.
  List those who make you feel good when <u>they</u>
  leave.

- Analyze those who make you feel good and decide
  why. Analyze those who make you feel bad and
  decide if you can avoid them. If you can't avoid
  them, decide what skills you will need to deal more
  positively with them.

SKILL

VIII

Learning to Grow from Adversity

ADVERSITY = CHALLENGE = OPPORTUNITY

Adversity is a challenge that provides an opportunity to learn and grow. There has been sufficient evidence to show how disaster can bring out the best in people.

Hurricanes, forest fires, earthquakes—all natural disasters—help people dig deep for strength and work together to overcome the ravages caused by the disaster.

The Oklahoma City disaster, which was caused by terrorists, rallied the whole country to action—
people responded,
> people pulled together,
>> people put their own lives on the line to help others,
>>> people helped people.

Disasters can be both devastating catastrophes and valuable learning opportunities for the people affected by them.

PERSONAL ADVERSITIES

Each person experiences adversity in life. What is adversity? Adversity, as defined in Webster's II New Riverside University Dictionary, is "a state of affliction or hardship; an instance of misfortune." Adversity is commonly defined as pain, suffering, hardship, misfortune, hurt, affliction, and tragedy. It can be defined differently by different people:

to some it is the death of a loved one;
to some it is a natural catastrophe;
to some it is the loss of a job;
to some it is alcohol or drug abuse.

Each form of adversity is a challenge to the person encountering the situation. Some adversities are difficult; some are tragic; some are short term; some are long term; some cause minor lifestyle changes; and some result in total upheaval of one's life. The one common element in adversity is the challenge presented to the individual.

Think of the challenges in your life—your natural disasters as opportunities to learn, to gain strength, to reach out for help, and to bring forth your best. This will help you to cope with surviving the trying times in your life.

PERSONAL TREASURE CHEST

Inside each person is a reservoir of strength, courage, and love reserved for those times when all resources seem to be exhausted. This reservoir is like a PERSONAL TREASURE CHEST hidden deep inside you, which contains unrealized skills, extra adrenaline, forgotten knowledge, deep love, and unbelievable strength. When faced with times of misfortune, we are forced to reach deep for courage, strength, love, and skills to meet the challenge. We dig into the buried resources found in our own PERSONAL TREASURE CHEST.

These extra resources arm us to confront and tackle the challenges and adversities encountered through life. They help us rise above the pain and suffering. At some time in your life, you have witnessed that inner vault of strength. Many a person perceived as a weak person performs heroic deeds in difficult times. People stand back and admire this new strength. They never see this person that way because they can't see the TREASURE CHEST deep inside each person.

Sometimes you don't think of yourself as a strong person and yet under pressure you can perform heroic deeds or help carry others through tumultuous times.

When I was nine months pregnant with my second child, we were living in an old house in Massachusetts. We had a washing machine but no dryer. One day I was outside hanging clothes on the line while my daughter, who was about 22 months old, was napping in an upstairs bedroom. It was cold and my fingers were freezing as I put clothespins on each garment. In the winter the clothes would actually freeze on the line to the point where they would stand up on the floor.

My daughter awoke and opened the window to wave at me. She climbed onto the window sill and was hanging half out the window. I ran upstairs with unbelievable speed and grabbed her feet just as she was falling out the window. How I ever got up those stairs when I was so pregnant and off balance was due to the strength and resources in my PERSONAL TREASURE CHEST.

I'm sure you can remember instances where your inner PERSONAL TREASURE CHEST gave you the power to perform extraordinary feats. Afterwards you wondered how you did it. People rise to the occasion by drawing strength, love, courage, and skills from their PERSONAL TREASURE CHEST.

ADVERSITY FOSTERS GROWTH

What does "grow from adversity" mean? Grow means to get bigger or become older, more mature, learn, or increase in size. You can grow physically, emotionally, intellectually, and spiritually. This growth happens as the result of life's experiences—good as well as bad experiences. Usually learning is more intense from adverse experiences. You learn from outpourings of love and pleasure, and joyous occasions, but if you think of life as a continuum, yardstick or growth line, you realize that you make giant steps forward emotionally, intellectually, and spiritually when you have adversity in your life. That is when you are forced to make decisions and take action which you would not do if you were in a comfortable situation.

DIFFERENT LEVELS OF ADVERSITY

Adversity has many levels of pain and suffering. Some adverse situations are simple challenges—a new job, for example, where you don't know anyone and you have to prove yourself again. You learn as you sharpen your skills, improve your attitude, and put your best foot forward to meet the challenge this opportunity has now presented.

Tragedies and catastrophes are more difficult challenges that push you forward at a faster pace. The more difficult the challenge the deeper you have to dig into your PERSONAL TREASURE CHEST—the inner vault—for strength. When you look at adversity as a challenge and opportunity, you can deal with the crisis more effectively.

The alternative is to fall apart and become a victim who complains, whines, and engages in pity parties; you can turn to alcohol or drugs—prescribed or illegal; you can flee hoping to outrun the unpleasant situation. Whatever your reaction, at some time you have to confront the situation, deal with it, and refocus your life.

In the Brooklyn apartment where I grew up, I lived with my mother and older sister. I never remember my father being in our home. He lived in that faraway and uncivilized Burbank, California. Today our home would be called a single parent home and we would be a statistic included in many studies. But when you are living the situation, you don't see yourself as a statistic. You are just trying to live.

I knew that other kids had fathers in their lives but that family structure had no meaning for me. When I visited my friends, I was always uncomfortable when their fathers came home, so I scheduled my visits when just their mother, brothers, or sisters were home. I found myself always quick to make excuses to leave if a father came home early.

Then there was always the untiring, wishful hope that my dad would come visit. He was a pioneer in the aviation industry and worked for many years at the Burbank airport. I am told that he was very intelligent. However, when we visited my grandfather and the other members of his large family, no one ever spoke about him. I would have liked to know more about him but I didn't want to cause additional pain for my mother, who was already suffering from loneliness.

One day he was supposedly coming to visit us. He was riding jump seat on an unscheduled transcontinental flight—a propeller-driven plane that was to land at La Guardia Field in New York. My mother, sister, and I took the subway to Queens and waited and waited. We waited for hours. I didn't even know what he would look like; I'd only seen photos. We waited and waited. He never came. It was a very long ride home that night on the subway. We didn't talk. There was no need. We shared the empty feeling without expressing a word.

This void in my life helped me to gain strength. Now I can look back and realize that I would not have been strong enough to survive other challenges in my life had I not gained strength from that early pain.

Not only was I the child of a single parent, but I was a child of a poor single parent. Again, I didn't know we were poor. I knew we were hungry and did not have money to buy clothes and frills. Our apartment was com-

fortable and the three of us shared a closeness that was cemented by both love and fear.

We always watched the mailbox for my father's check which was barely enough to pay the rent and always late. My mother would plead with the landlord to be patient. He always was because we didn't cause any trouble. My aunt also lived in the apartment building and he liked both her and my mother. He always gave us time because we didn't cause any trouble.

Because we were afraid of making the landlord mad, many times we froze rather than complain about the lack of heat. I remember many nights freezing in bed with flannel sheets, flannel pajamas and two blankets. Other people would bang on the radiators at night. The banging was in protest to the landlord. He didn't like it. We never banged. We didn't want to disturb the landlord or make him mad. We would always lay low — never ask questions, never rock the boat. I learned that lesson well.

It was at this time in my life that fear and guilt were deeply embedded in me. Fear and apprehension stayed with me for many years, but I finally learned to take my power back. I learned that fear and apprehension were just conditions of the mind that can be controlled. I learned that I had the right to rock the boat, the right to ask questions. I finally learned — it's my job!

When my mother went to work at the ribbon counter at McCrory's, we had steady money. Around my neck I wore a long metal key, which was very cold in the winter, so that I could get into our apartment after school. Today I would be labeled with a derogatory name — latch-key child. I didn't know I was a latchkey kid. I didn't mind being a latchkey kid. It allowed us to have the food and clothes we needed, and a few less worries. I went to meet my mother at the subway every night. I played games with other kids there. The only difference was that they were waiting for their fathers. There was always a crowd, because the majority of people who lived where I lived used the subway for transportation.

We learned to use our money frugally. We went everywhere by subway for a nickel. We went to the big museums in Manhattan where we learned about history, science, geography, different cultures, and art. Hence, my burning love for history and museums. We went to the Bronx Zoo where we learned about animals and fell in love with giant pandas before they became popular. Hence, my love for zoos, which I visit whenever I can. We went to the beach where we learned about the ocean. Hence, my passionate love for the ocean and my compelling desire to walk along the shore and wonder about the powerful yet soothing sea. We used the public libraries where we learned about the power of reading to open new horizons. Hence, my obsessive drive to read five books at a time.

This was my childhood. I didn't know I was a single parent child, though I knew my father was absent from home. I didn't know I was poor, though I knew I was hungry and at times cold. I didn't know I was a latchkey child, though I knew my mother worked, which helped us and so I was proud of her. I didn't know about labels—I learned from the hardships rather than succumbing to them. I learned to create a mystique. I lived in that mystique. That mystique gave me PRIDE and I was very proud.

I learned from those experiences and drew strength beyond belief. I learned about people. We lived in a true melting pot among many different ethnic groups and newly arrived immigrants speaking different languages. This is why many people who are raised in a ghetto or barrio, or just in poverty itself, rise above the situation. They are the ones who learned from the experience and didn't get mired in the mud of their surroundings. This is a skill that can be learned to help people escape dreadful surroundings. Most people don't realize they are part of society's labels; they just live there and that is their norm.

PEOPLE NEED SKILLS—NOT LABELS

Remember **precept number one: Each Person Is Doing His or Her Best.** Not many people get up in the morning planning to ruin their life, mess up their children, or perform poorly at work or school. When you deeply believe this principle of life, then you can understand why it is so important to teach skills needed to grow from adversity. Instead of labeling and giving money and food stamps to people living in poverty—
give them skills,
give them education,
give them work,
give them pride.
Stop taking away their dignity by giving them handouts. It doesn't help.

When I was in high school, my mother decided to leave New York City to move to New England where we had family. Since I had finished eighth grade in January—we had half-year classes in Brooklyn—I needed to skip one semester of high school. When I started high school, the cliques were already in place. I didn't know anyone and was also missing a semester. It was a miserable beginning to high school, one of the most difficult times in my life.

My mother worked in a nursing home. As we had no place to live, we moved into the top floor of the nursing home. It was a very good home and patients received loving care there, but it smelled like sickness and death all the time.

When I came home from a date, my boyfriend (who I later married) would drop me at the side door. I could never invite anyone to my room. I was too humiliated. I would climb the stairs with that awful smell around me, moaning and groaning sounds coming from the rooms. At the top of the stairs was my room, a small hospital-size room with a metal bed and dresser.

In the morning I ate in the employees' dining room. I ate hospital food, usually dry toast and scrambled eggs made in a huge pan with very little seasoning. The staff would talk about the patients and their health problems. Somehow I always managed to lose my appetite during their conversations.

The people were very nice and cared about me, but I hated it there. I always felt the few clothes I had smelled like sickness and death. I would walk to school hoping the air would cleanse my skin and clothes.

We had no television and as a matter of fact I grew up pretty much without television — that was not all bad. However, the kids at school had televisions and they would talk about different programs. But then they were different. They had fathers. They had clothes. They had real homes. I didn't belong. I was never part of any group. But I was smart and excelled at my studies. Hence, my passion for the academic world.

These depressing surroundings challenged me as a teenager to do better. College had to wait temporarily. I didn't want four more years of sacrifice. I wanted to earn money. I wanted a home. I wanted real food. I wanted clothes. I wanted perfume, room fresheners, and potpourri. I wanted nice smells around me.

These childhood times were adverse but created powerful learning experiences for me. They gave me strength. They taught me tolerance, love, and respect for people; they taught me pride and responsibility. They taught me to identify my talents and use them; they taught me the value of learning and the purpose of life. So many lessons in so few years.

ADVERSITY ADVANCES LEARNING

You grow at a certain rate and then there is a surge, usually connected to a difficult situation in your life. You can tell how many surges you have had by reviewing your life.

For example, I was an excellent student and received mostly A's. This was an area of my life that I could control. I worked hard and was not accustomed to receiving B's. Then I came across a writing professor in college who was formidable.

It was a writing class and I disliked writing. I worked hard and got a B. I was so upset because I didn't get an A. However, I learned more in that class than in most other classes in which I received higher grades. That teacher taught me the value of writing as a form of expression. Now I write all the time. You do learn from the challenges in your life.

You learn as you grow just by being another year older, but you definitely learn more from the challenges. When you have to work hard and dig for the strength, you use all your talents and skills.

EVERY DAY IS LIKE A CARD GAME

Life is like a continual card game. In a card game, sometimes you are dealt aces and sometimes you are dealt two's, three's, or even jokers. You have to play the cards you are dealt for that hand. You get new cards in the next hand. Sometimes you get an awesome hand and sometimes you get a real bummer. Most of the time you get an average hand. However, you have to play all hands. It takes more skill, effort, and patience to play the poor hand but when you win it is even more exciting and rewarding than winning with a strong hand.

I decided to get my long-awaited college education. However, it was not to be an easy start. Challenges came flooding my way. Sometimes challenges are tests to see if you want something bad enough.

My mother became seriously ill with cancer. Her treatment was to be surgery followed by deep x-ray therapy for four weeks. This particular radiation was only available in a hospital, which was about thirty-five miles away. I withdrew from school and my mother, three kids and I made the trek for thirty days. She made good progress and her treatment was completed in a month. Fortunately, she made a complete recovery. She decided to take a much-needed vacation and visit her sister in New York the following week. The children and I took her to the airport and upon returning home received a telephone call.

It seemed that my father was dying and I was the next of kin responsible for him. I found that ironic, as he had never been responsible for me. I was scheduled to go to the hospital the next morning, but he died during the night. It became my job to bury a man I truly did not know.

He was a nice man. He was a smart man. He was definitely my father, as I looked just like him. I didn't know him but I loved him. I wish I had known him, as he led a fascinating life. He was brave, fearless, and a major risk-taker. He had all the qualities I lacked. I could have learned many things from him that would have made my life easier. Instead, I learned them through mistakes and a lot of pain.

In life you are dealt cards to play every day. Sometimes they are good cards: good health, financial security, pleasant surroundings, fun experiences—the good times. Sometimes they are terrible cards: sickness, accidents, violence, disasters, and tragedies—the bad times. Most of the time they are comfortable cards with a few minor problems—the normal times.

Whatever combination of cards you are dealt, they are yours until you receive new cards. The challenge is to play them the best you can. Maybe you don't have a royal flush (the best hand in poker), maybe you don't have a full house (a very good hand in poker), maybe you don't have a single pair and the highest card in your hand is a seven (a bummer hand in poker), but that is what you have today and you have to make the best of that hand. Maybe tomorrow you will be dealt a royal flush. We all have royal flush days. Those are the days to celebrate.

Those are the days to build the reservoir in your PERSONAL TREASURE CHEST by adding to your supply. When you restock your PERSONAL TREASURE CHEST you can be ready when you are dealt a bummer hand. We grow from both hands—but we grow by leaps and bounds from the bad ones.

FILL YOUR PERSONAL TREASURE CHEST

Life is always in transition from good experiences to bad experiences and back again. That is why we have good days and bad days. The bad times help us appreciate the good times, and yet we take the good times for granted. Be joyous when you, your family, and friends are doing well and feeling fine! Be thankful! Enjoy the respite!

Good times allow time to restock your PERSONAL TREASURE CHEST hidden deep inside. Replenish love by building, sharing, and enjoying the company of friends and family. These are the people who will be there for you during adversity. Build the relationships now to have when you are faced with the bad times, struggles, and hardships. Build your support base during the good times.

•GAIN STRENGTH BY APPRECIATING THE WORLD AND BEAUTY AROUND YOU•

•ABSORB THE ENJOYABLE EXPERIENCES•

•LISTEN TO THE ENTERTAINING MUSIC•

•HAVE FUN•

•CHERISH YOUR WORLD•

Then when you encounter adversity, you will be ready with a full reservoir to tackle the serious challenges.

This approach certainly does not mean to expect or invite calamities, catastrophes, or other ill-boding times into your life. It simply means to be prepared—emotionally, physically, intellectually, and spiritually—so you can be effective during the bad times of your life and make the best decisions.

The sudden death of my husband was the most difficult time of my life. I went through the motions but I truly don't remember the details. I remember the children screaming in disbelief. I remember sitting outside in the air wondering what happened.

I remember my wonderful children and their spouses and how we all pulled together and supported and nurtured each other. I remember my friends and family who were there for me that night and after. Thirty-two years and nothing was left. My life was at a standstill. It was a shock. By pulling my children through this tragic event, I pulled myself through the unbelievable anguish.

You don't always control adversity but you do control your responses to the challenge. They can be opportunities to move leaps and bounds on that growth line or they can be totally disastrous to you as a person. The choice is yours. When you fill your PERSONAL TREASURE CHEST with—
support,
   inner strength,
      skills,
         courage,
            peace,
               beauty,
                  and love,
you will make it through the most difficult times. Then you will survive, emerge stronger, and move on to the royal flush days.

ALLOW TIME FOR THE PAIN

Always give yourself time to suffer when you deal with pain and adversity. This pain can be released through tears, prayer, counseling, reading, or whatever helps you. My way of dealing with adversity is to have a conversation with God. I frequently have words with God, and sometimes I get angry and really cry out in frustration. I choose God because He understands me—He forgives me and loves me. Therefore, when I am angry, I choose to express my anger and outrage in whatever language brings me relief. (I always tell people to tell God I sent them, that He will know who I am because we have many heart-to-heart talks.) Sometimes these talks are through tears, sometimes they are very quiet and sometimes they are loud, but I always feel better because He comforts and understands me.

This way I don't need to apologize to anyone. People have long memories and if you do or say something negative, angry, crude, or stupid they don't forget and always remind you of your weakness. Yet we all need an outlet. For me there is no better outlet than someone who knows me intimately and is responsible for my very being. When we are angry we say things that can be hurtful. God alone understands us—mouth and all. He knows our gifts, talents, strengths, weaknesses, and personality.

One time, I was living in Phoenix, when everything was going wrong in my life. I was still recovering from my husband's death, my oldest son had become ill, and my grandson was also ill with a rare disease.

In ten days my son was having surgery, I was scheduled to attend a five-day seminar in California, I had to return my car to my employer and purchase one, make a trip to Washington, D.C. for a two-day conference, and attend one day of drivers school for a speeding ticket.

I went to California on Sunday to check into my seminar. On Monday morning my son had an operation. For the next five days I went to my seminar every morning and then drove thirty-five miles to the hospital where I stayed until ten o'clock. I then drove back to Los Angeles to the hotel and read my material for the next day. On Friday I returned home to Phoenix.

I didn't have a car so I rented one at the airport. I was standing there with three heavy bags at 11:30PM and my car was in the last stall at the very end of the ramp. My feet hurt and it was over 110 degrees. I looked down the aisle and saw how far I had to walk to get to my car.

I stood there becoming angrier by the minute and then I finally decided to have a conversation with God. I told Him what I thought about all these challenges. I finally was yelling at the top of my lungs — "I've had enough opportunities and challenges. When do I get some peace?"

This very handsome gentleman came over and offered to help me with my bags. I thanked him and assured him I was fine, just expressing my frustrations. I picked up my bags and went to the car. I spent the next day in drivers school, thanking God for this wonderful opportunity to rest.

Since then I have learned to say, "Thank you, God, for this opportunity." It doesn't mean that I'm not unhappy. It doesn't mean that I don't cry. It doesn't mean that I don't have my own pity parties. We all need to release our hurt, anger, and pain. I choose someone to whom I don't have to apologize.

These conversations are timely and over quickly. I don't need to schedule an appointment or meet in an uncomfortable place. These conversations allow me to move forward again. This is an effective use of venting. Everyone needs an outlet as long as it doesn't become a crutch. No one who is healthy and free needs a crutch to walk. Crutches are for those who can't walk. For those able to walk they become a handicap or impediment to progress.

REVITALIZE THROUGH INSPIRATION

The best way to get inspiration for your own life is to focus on those who are dealing with tragedies in their life in a positive way. These people can be a beacon for those who are newly challenged. People like Christopher Reeve who, paralyzed from a freak accident, has dug deep for inner strength and hidden resources to continue his life and seek a new direction for his talents.

Visit the ward of a hospital where people are suffering from catastrophic illness or linked to respirators for the very breath of life. Visit those who are blind or paralyzed. Read the life stories of heroic people. There are stories, insights, and lessons for learning. What powerful tools these stories can be! What powerful CLASSROOMS OF LEARNING! There are many books available in the library or at the bookstore. Look in the inspiration or biography section. It will certainly give you hope and a feeling of optimism. We all need encouragement at times. It is as close as your nearest hospital, bookstore, or library.

HELP OTHERS TO HELP YOURSELF

When faced with a traumatic or disastrous situation in your life, you can best help yourself by helping others endure the same challenge. As you help them, you automatically pull yourself through the same misfortune. If you don't know how to get through an illness, the death of a loved one or other tragedy, find someone who needs help getting through the same tragedy. Help that person and you will pull yourself through without realizing what you are doing. Helping others forces you to reach into that PERSONAL TREASURE CHEST to find the needed strength, courage, love, and skills to overcome the most difficult times.

FACE THE CHALLENGES DIRECTLY

I was scared when I left Brooklyn, but I met my husband in New England. I was scared when I left New England, but I received my education and started my career in California. I was scared when I left California, but my career blossomed in Colorado. I was scared when I left Colorado, but my career flourished in Arizona. I was scared when my husband died, but I became a new person.

Each time I have had a challenge I have dug deep for the strength to meet it. How appropriate to write this book in Phoenix, named after the mythical bird who rose from the ashes. How coincidental! I have risen from the ashes many times. You can overcome tremendous adversity if you see it as a challenge. This is not an easy task—some catastrophes take years to overcome, some you never forget. But you learn to cope.

START FILLING YOUR

PERSONAL TREASURE

CHEST TODAY!

LESSONS

- Identify family members and friends who can serve as a support group for your PERSONAL TREASURE CHEST.

- Work to build positive and caring relationships with the family members and friends you have identified.

- Make a list of available resources to have ready when you need help. This can include clergy, counselors, support groups, social agencies, hot lines, etc.

- Read an inspirational book and highlight certain passages and quotations that you can refer to in time of need.

- Search for inspirational pamphlets or booklets which you can keep readily available in times of need. These can be religious, spiritual, or even poetry.

SKILL

IX

Learning to Adapt to Change

ACCELERATION OF CHANGE

Change is all around us. The world as our ancestors knew it two hundred years ago is gone. The world as we knew it twenty-five years, even five years ago is gone. The world as we knew it yesterday is gone. Tomorrow's world is unknown. It is even more necessary to be the *Leader of Yourself* in this rapidly changing world than it was in the world five, twenty-five or a hundred years ago. It can be argued that life was simpler then. Maybe that's why people refer to the past as the good old days.

Conducting business was easier and less stressful. Consider the decision-making skills needed to buy a car at the time when Henry Ford was quoted as saying, "You can have any color car as long as it is black." It was a far cry from the skills needed to buy a car today. There are numerous makes, models, accessories, and buying plans available.

Maybe the reason life seemed more predictable in the past was because hindsight is always better—you have more information. It is easy to make a decision after all facts are known. It is more difficult when there are many unknown factors or changing variables. When you look at life through the lenses of the past, the rapid change swirling around you validates the need for skills to adapt to change. It is critical that you become involved in change. You cannot just drift and exist. The change will spin around you and snatch you like a tornado. The only way to manage change is to be a *Leader of Yourself* and enthusiastically participate in the change.

MANY LITTLE CORNERS OF THE WORLD = THE BIG PICTURE

You can't stop the changes happening around you. But you can be a major player in directing the outcome of these changes. This is true not only in your little corner of the world but in the big picture as well. The big picture is the sum of all the little corners of the world. When there are true leaders in each little corner of the world, the big picture will be reflective of the desires and wishes of the little corners.

For example, if educators better prepared students in economics, geography, and science, maybe there would not be the huge federal budget deficit or the environmental issues we face today. The truth is, most people do not realize how government gets and spends money. Suddenly there is a huge deficit. A *Leader of Yourself* can monitor and guide the economy by thoughtful selection of leaders. A *Leader of Yourself* asks questions—not from an emotionally hyped perspective but from a knowledge base.

INDUSTRY CHANGE

The hotel industry, banking industry, health care industry, restaurant industry, retail industry, automobile industry, airline industry, communication industry, food industry, entertainment industry, and electronic industry, all have undergone dramatic changes. Words such as downsizing, restructuring, consolidation, and buyouts, are frequently used in the media.

Each of those industries includes others dependent on the core industry. For example, dependent on the automobile industry are gas stations, car washes, and automobile part stores. When you think of the possible products, services, and jobs involved under each core industry, it really becomes mind-boggling. If you are not employed in one of these industries, you are probably a client or customer. It is difficult to find someone who is not directly or indirectly involved with each of these industries.

AUTOMOBILE INDUSTRY

In the sixties, the little Volkswagen Beetle came to popularity. These little *bugs* ran all over the place. They were inexpensive to purchase and economical to run. They were different from American-made cars. They caught on and changed the automobile industry. Soon *bugs* were followed by Toyotas, Datsuns, and other cars. All these cars were basic, inexpensive, got good gas mileage, and had favorable track records for low maintenance. They did not have the luxuries of the American-made cars. They were different. They were novel. They were exciting. They sold like hotcakes.

What they really did was challenge the automobile industry in this country. That challenge forced our automobile manufacturers to rethink designs, maintenance, and even the accessories to be included in cars. At first, the result was very depressing, as plants shut down to be retooled, automated, consolidated, or closed. These plants were closed in reaction to the little Beetle and its new style of car. The end product today is a better American-made car. American-made cars now offer a combination of luxury, economy, and efficiency.

A year of long gas lines resulted in the purchase of our first foreign compact car designed to get 30 to 40 miles to the gallon. My husband was so proud of this "cute little car." He liked the way it handled—he liked the little tires that would be so reasonable to replace.

We were going on a Christmas vacation to the mountains with some friends. We had to take the "cute little car" because it was new and would be easy to drive on the windy mountain roads. So we packed and prepared for our trip. It soon became obvious that luggage for six people, including one toddler, would not fit in the "cute little car's" trunk. No problem. Our friends could put the extra luggage in their station wagon.

Next, we proceeded to put the kids in the car—the toddler on a booster and two others in the back. The front had those neat bucket seats, so of course only two adults could fit there. My husband was so proud that there was plenty of room. The only problem was that our teenage daughter was still in the house. I looked over and asked where she was to ride. You guessed it. The kids were packed in the back like sardines and I held the toddler on my lap for the two-and-one-half hour drive. It was a "cute little car!"

Let's look at the changes in gas stations. Attendants used to fill the tank, clean windows, check oil, or even put air in tires. Stations had several mechanics on hand to fix a tire or do maintenance on your car. Then came self-service pumps in regular service stations. Then came service centers sometimes found on each corner of an intersection. Next service centers merged with convenience stores and became one-stop centers. Now you can insert money into a pump and fill your car without seeing a person. What's next—alternative fuel centers for electric cars, or propane cars? These changes are designed to meet the needs of a fast-moving society where people want to get in and out, not pass the time of day—
different scenario,
   different times,
      changing needs!

BANKING INDUSTRY

Examine the continual transformation in the banking industry. I can remember when there was only one branch of a bank and it was downtown. The atmosphere was extremely quiet and somber. The bank was traditionally open from 9:00AM to 3:00PM every day during the week.

When suburbs started growing, along came branch banking. Then came branch banking with drive-thrus equipped with tellers. Next came the computerized ATM without tellers, followed by drive-thrus with no tellers. ATM's are open 24 hours a day and a very convenient and efficient way of doing business.

Touch tone phones make it easy for a customer to transfer, deposit, withdraw money, pay loans, order checks, or whatever. Computers can now be used to pay bills and conduct normal banking functions. Plastic in the form of debit cards replaces the need for cash. As competition increases, banks merge, thus consolidating and closing branch offices. Bankers who worked twenty years ago would not recognize the business today. These changes are designed to meet the needs of a fast-moving society that does not want to wait in line for service.

This is a challenge for the banking industry because increased services that are convenient are moving banks to grocery stores, shopping malls, and even airports, at the same time neighborhood branches are being closed. Hurry! Hurry! Hurry! Just like the March Hare in Alice in Wonderland—
I'm late—I'm late—I'm late,
speed up—speed up—speed up,
change—change—change.

RETAIL INDUSTRY

This industry is in a continual metamorphosis. For many years the downtown department store in a city was the focal point of the retail business. As suburbs grew, shopping malls with department stores as anchors were built. Malls stayed open evenings and Sundays. This helped cause the demise of the downtown stores, which were usually open one night and not on Sunday, except at Christmas time.

About the same time, along came K-Mart. When discount stores first opened, they weren't taken seriously because most of the products were low quality. However, they did sell some brand-name items, such as appliances. Soon department stores stopped selling appliances. Then more discount stores opened and they captured more markets such as toys, sporting goods, and electronics. Soon department stores stopped selling those lines.

Now traditional shopping malls are being replaced by outlet malls, power malls, or destination malls. The first outlet malls held products and goods that did not sell or were left on the racks. Now outlet stores also carry a regular merchandise line and are very popular. Power malls are comprised of large specialty establishments like housewares and linens stores, computer equipment stores, electronic stores, office products stores, toy stores, and clothing stores. Even one of the last holdouts to change— the lucrative cosmetic industry—is changing. This highly competitive industry is selling its products in power mall stores, outlet stores, and even grocery stores. All of these changes have been made to accommodate the needs of a fast-moving society—a society that wants wide selection and value.

THE LIST GOES ON

Anyone who has visited a doctor's office or hospital recently has seen the visible changes in the health care industry. HMO, PPO, primary care physician, pre-certification are all terms new to patients. Many good doctors are retiring because they feel they are compromising the health of their patients. While their concern is justified, their retirement will not slow down changes in health care.

Many of you have experienced problems in the health care industry yourself, or have family or friends who have encountered unnecessary problems in difficult health times. Yet how many of you have any input to the changes? You are just the patient! You are just the client! What do you know about health care? **Change— Change—Change!**

THRIVE DURING CHANGE

Volumes have been written on the downsizing, restructuring, reorganizing, redesigning, and retooling of these particular industries as well as numerous others not mentioned here. They all have the same ramifications for us. It is difficult to see the outcome when you are in the middle of the change. This is where the skill of vision is needed to guide the process.

Unfortunately, we have been led to believe that this skill is held only by a select few, when in fact you can develop this skill with practice. Remember: **practice— practice—practice**. Isn't it better to participate in the solution even though it means total change? At least you can help guide the change. A *Leader of Yourself* will not only survive but actively participate in this rapidly changing society.

HOLDER OF THE LEASH

Picture someone walking a dog. Who is in control? Who is on the leash? Sometimes it feels as if we are being pulled at a fast pace to an unknown destination. The scenery is changing so rapidly around us that it seems to be on fast-forward speed. It is a true runaway situation. That's where we are with technology.

> *My first job after graduating from high school was as a key punch operator at an insurance company. I punched cards all day and then filed them. There were huge machines that were wired using big boards with lots of wires. I learned how to wire them for simple sorting projects.*
>
> *I never dreamed that this job was the beginning of a sophisticated computer technology. I was on the ground floor of a burgeoning industry and I didn't even know it. I was not afraid of technology, just unaware of the change happening right around me.*

Technology is changing fast, and if we are not actively involved or have the skills to react to new technology, we will remain victims in a reactionary mode. The dog on the leash is our fast-moving society and technology is holding the leash. This picture needs to be reversed. People must lead and guide technology. The inability to assume that role will lower our quality of life, or at the extreme be the demise of the human side of our society.

PERSONALIZE THE CHANGE

Take a close personal look at each of the industries and review the changes you have experienced for yourself. Next, look at the change that has occurred in your lifetime. Look at music, plays, books—music, drama and literature have consistently changed through the years, but there has never been this massive explosion of the numbers of books, plays, and music produced. The broadening scope of knowledge, ideas, theories, and perspectives available to you, the customer, is overwhelming and growing exponentially. Next, determine the most effective way for you to get involved in the change—the most effective way for you to become a player in the game of life.

We owned one of the first television computer games — pong. Our family played pong for hours. We watched this simple ball go back and forth across the screen and tried to direct it with a paddle. This was analogous to watching a test pattern on early television. Today's graphics on television computer games are awesome and far advanced from pong.

My computer skills were limited to video games. However, when I decided to write, I purchased a computer, carried it home, and assembled it. I was overjoyed when the screen lit up when I turned on the switch. I knew there was hope for me.

I posted the 800 number by my computer and diligently began the tutorial program. I proceeded to learn how to operate the computer with the instruction manual close at hand. Once I became involved in learning the computer, new information and uses opened up to me.

•YOU LEARN WHAT YOU WANT•

•YOU LEARN WHEN YOU PROVIDE YOURSELF THE OPPORTUNITY•

CHANGE FOSTERS INSECURITY

Change can produce the unsettling feeling known as insecurity. This insecurity fuels fear and causes a reaction that tries to block change. For example, in many offices, as the management installed computers, office employees delayed or even refused to learn how to operate them. They boycotted the advancement of technology, sometimes in a silent way. However, as people left the company or retired, job descriptions were changed to include skills in operating a computer or, at the very least, a willingness to learn the new technology.

Because of fear, those already employed, who possibly had the best ideas about how to make the most efficient and effective use of the new technology, were pushed out of jobs. If they had learned the skills to overcome this fear, they could have led the change and designed a smooth transition to technology.

Secretaries are particularly vulnerable to this phenomenon. Here is an opportunity to raise the salary levels of a profession that has been a low-paid career because it is basically female-dominated. Secretaries either have not addressed the issue or have settled for status quo, instead of embracing the change as a way to showcase their talents and increased responsibilities. Voice mail, e-mail, fax machines, and other technological advances have helped secretaries and office personnel to restructure their jobs. As duties change, compensation can be reviewed in light of greater value to the organization. Many offices have dramatically changed secretarial job descriptions and restructured the management of their operations.

While we may argue that voice mail is important, it is part of the impersonal technology problem. Maybe if secretaries had been holding the leash, they would have implemented voice mail differently. It might not have been so impersonal and accepted in the business world without a struggle. Maybe if secretaries had been more involved in holding the leash they could have guaranteed a smoother transition. It may look different than it does today. You don't stop change by boycotting or blocking but rather you become a *Leader of Yourself* who learns new skills and guides the change process. It's time to start holding the leash.

INCLUSION OF EVERYONE

It is absolutely critical to include the total population in this exciting technological transformation. This must be an inclusive, not an exclusive, revolution. The only way to accomplish this task is to educate our total population. Computers and other technology must be made available through libraries, schools, and community centers. This is as necessary and valuable to society as rapid transit or environmental issues. It is imperative that all people be included.

INVASION OF PRIVACY

The technological revolution is threatening the privacy issue. As you go to sign on the Internet, you may wonder if your credit card information is displayed across the country. I beam with excitement when I see the tiny new home computers. I shake with trepidation when I give private information on the computer screen. Telephones are another example of the privacy issue; but then telephones have always been a challenge to me.

When I was living in California I once got a job in a typing pool so that I could spend time with my husband as he commuted to Santa Monica for three months. One day I was sent upstairs to Mahogany Row at Douglas Aircraft to substitute for an executive secretary who was ill. Due to a series of coincidences, all of the executive secretaries were out of the office at one time.

I had never been near Mahogany Row. You only dream of the beautiful offices, the well-dressed people, the very expensive suits, the power of the executives. The latest telephone equipment was reserved for those who worked there.

My job was to answer the phone and get coffee. I was to be there for three days. I lasted only one day because I didn't know how to use the hold button on the telephone. After disconnecting a General in the Pentagon three times, I had a new understanding of the term "three strikes and you're out."

I kept trying to figure out this impressive looking system. It had so many buttons — confidential buttons, hold buttons, personal buttons, intercom buttons. It had private lines, in-house lines, outside lines, and watts lines. There was neither an instruction manual nor a person to ask. I didn't have a clue so I learned by trial and error. The result was disaster!

I often wonder about all those privacy buttons with the advent of cellular systems. These convenient telephones can be menacing, because people can monitor your conversations if they choose. I thought that telephones were private. They were always available for creative folks who knew how to tap your line and listen. It is just more common to listen now. The bottom line is that cellular phones meet the needs of a fast-moving society that must be available and respond immediately.

QUALITY OF LIFE ISSUES

What happens to quality of life during these technological advances? There is another perspective to the privacy issue, that of being disturbed. Have you ever been in a restaurant and heard several phones ring or pagers beep? Have you ever attended a play and heard a phone ring at a poignant part? These are invasions of privacy.

Quality of life concerns need to be raised in the developmental stages of technology. But, as usual, most of us don't know things are happening until they already have. You can't influence anything if you don't know it is happening. You can't influence anything if you are afraid of it. Skeptics can stick their heads in the sand, but the changes will continue.

CHANGE IN GOVERNMENT

Government institutions have not changed, government has not changed. This could be part of the discontent of the people. Politicians are still operating business as usual, unaware of the changes swirling around them. They have not reexamined their positions as to the needs of today's society. Much public policy is outdated and desperately in need of revision. This is an arena where the general population needs education. Many people do not know what public policy is or how they can influence the development of policy, just as they don't know how the deficit grew to such high numbers. Public policy needs to be brought in line with the needs of the fast-moving society that wants immediate response and action.

When you are the *Leader of Yourself* you will question public policy from an issue basis and not an emotional basis. You then become an effective mover in your community. Influencing public policy will force government institutions to change. This is probably the only realistic way that government institutions, including schools, will change. Industries became more productive when competition forced change. Government institutions lack competition and thus survive despite incompetence or obsolescence.

ENJOY AND LEARN FROM CHANGE

Change is not to be feared, but rather enjoyed; effective change will improve your life. Learn new skills— don't hide, don't be defensive.

My first college class, at a community college, was a health class. What an education! Sister Mary Anita, my high school teacher, never taught health like that. The professor said that women who were supported by their husbands were parasites. I didn't see it that way as I cleaned house, washed and ironed clothes, made meals, and took care of our most prized possessions, the children.

But this was the sixties and things were changing. I remember being very offended at her remark. I became defensive and rationalized that, as she had never been married, she had no understanding of my job. I made it through that class and learned a lot about different points of view. I realized how sheltered my education had been.

That experience prepared me for college life later in the sixties when everything was challenged, when there were sit-ins at the administrative center, offensive art displays that were projects for master degrees, and unrest in general. This was a long distance from Sister Mary Anita. I was in a new world and struggling to stay an active participant. Many students who were my age and returning from a homemaker environment quit and stayed home. I often wonder how much talent and how many future contributions were missed by society because these frightened people were afraid of change.

The sixties gave students a total education in change. Although there was no class titled *Change 101*, there was change in every classroom, dining hall, student union, and corner of the colleges and universities.

There were times when I almost quit because of the rebellious events on campus. I enrolled in a writing class. The professor returned my first assignment with a D. Never having received a D grade in school, I went to his office to seek help.

The professor said that my work was not expressive because it lacked four-letter words, and unless I was willing to include obscene language in my writing he would continue to give me low grades. I dropped the class. He said I didn't really belong to the changing world.

He was a genuine real live hippie professor so tolerant of mankind, fighting for civil rights. I didn't belong because I wouldn't use four-letter words. I always wondered what had happened to my civil rights and freedom of expression.

Our society needs everyone guiding and participating in these changes from the developmental level. Technology is moving too fast. Human development is not keeping pace. You are a part of society. Isn't it better to learn skills and participate in the changes? Isn't it important to lend your uniqueness and ideas to the changes before they are finalized? Can't you see you could be the missing link that society needs to maintain a good quality of life?

We live in a throwaway world, a world without stability. A world that is scary. A world we sometimes would like to slow down but, as hard as we try, changes faster and faster. Participation must be encouraged and welcomed.

•A LEADER OF YOURSELF IS NOT AFRAID OF CHANGE•

> *•A LEADER OF YOURSELF IS AN ACTIVE, VIBRANT PART OF CHANGE•*

> > *•A LEADER OF YOURSELF GUIDES CHANGE TO INSURE QUALITY OF LIFE•*

HOLD THE LEASH OF

CHANGE, TO INSURE

QUALITY OF LIFE!

LESSONS

- Review the changes you have experienced in two industries. Identify the improvement or problems in your life as a result of these changes.

- Stop and reflect on what the world looked like one hundred years ago. Think of the changes to the environment and the life of the people who sat where you are sitting right now.

- Make a list of technological equipment about which you have minimal information. Develop a plan to increase your knowledge about this technology.

- Make a list of the changes occurring in your corner of the world that cause you concern or fear.

- Make a list of changes that could occur in your corner of the world to improve your quality of life. Identify the person or organization to which you could submit your list of proposed changes.

- Read a book by a leading futurist that will cause you to reflect on the changes facing society in the future.

- Visualize and discuss with family members or friends what you foresee in your life in five years and twenty-five years.

SKILL

X

Learning to Embrace Commitment

COMMITMENT = PURPOSE IN LIFE

Commitment gives you a purpose in life. Purpose in life explains why you live. Do you actually believe you just happened on the scene? No, you came into this world for a purpose. This purpose is your very reason for existence. The people, issues, career, ideas, and values to which you are committed define you. They are right in front of you. The sum total of your commitments equals your purpose in life. This purpose is different for each person. That is why each person has mastered each skill at different levels.

INVENTORY YOUR PURPOSE IN LIFE

If you are unsure of your purpose in life, take an inventory of your surroundings, relationships, and involvement with people, projects, work, hobbies, clubs, organizations, school, and churches. This will catalog your current purpose in life. This purpose in life can change as you learn more skills, WIDEN YOUR PERSPECTIVES, encounter more experiences, and generally increase your awareness of your surroundings.

EMBRACING A COMMITMENT

Now that you have learned the other nine skills, it is time to apply them to **Embracing a Commitment.** This skill requires using the prior skills—to formulate ideas, positions, and statements, to develop beliefs, to take action by getting involved, to nurture and support yourself and others.

It requires you to determine—
what you believe,
    what you value,
        with whom you want to have relation-
        ships,
            where you want to focus your
            energies,
                how you want to allocate
                your most precious asset,
                your time.

•*TIME IS YOUR MOST IMPORTANT RESOURCE*•

•*TIME CANNOT BE PURCHASED*•

•*TIME CANNOT BE SLOWED DOWN*•

•*TIME CANNOT BE RELIVED*•

COMPLEX OR SIMPLE

Life is confusing and profound, or is it? Is it really quite simple, but we complicate it? Is it complex, and we try to simplify it? Interesting paradox. Which comes first, the simplicity or the complexity? Many times we are our own worst enemy.

My introduction to philosophy was through the study of Plato. The class discussion centered around the difference between an idea and an object. The conversation focused on the belief that a chair existed only because the idea of a chair existed. I was totally bewildered by that point of view. I remember saying to my classmate, this idea I am sitting on is very hard. I missed the whole point of the discussion.

What is reality and what is illusion? What is complex and what is simple?

INVENTORY OF SKILLS

In order to develop skills needed to embrace commitments, you need to inventory your mastery of the nine skills listed previously. Place yourself on the following scales according to your own assessment.

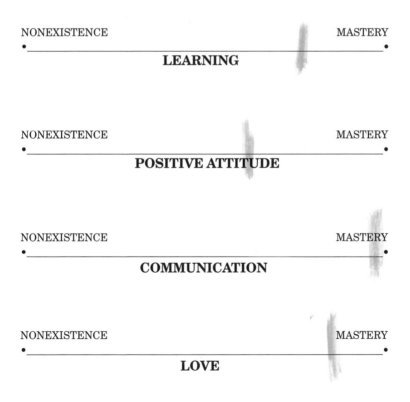

NONEXISTENCE   MASTERY

LEARNING

NONEXISTENCE   MASTERY

POSITIVE ATTITUDE

NONEXISTENCE   MASTERY

COMMUNICATION

NONEXISTENCE   MASTERY

LOVE

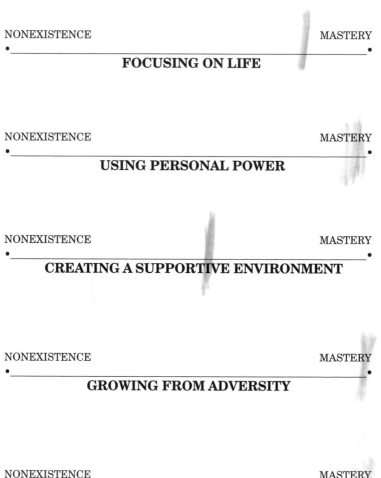

NONEXISTENCE   MASTERY

•—————————————————————————————•

FOCUSING ON LIFE

NONEXISTENCE   MASTERY

•—————————————————————————————•

USING PERSONAL POWER

NONEXISTENCE   MASTERY

•—————————————————————————————•

CREATING A SUPPORTIVE ENVIRONMENT

NONEXISTENCE   MASTERY

•—————————————————————————————•

GROWING FROM ADVERSITY

NONEXISTENCE   MASTERY

•—————————————————————————————•

ADAPTING TO CHANGE

You can expect to be further on the continuum in some skills than in others. Some are easier for you than others. Remember: You need all **ten skills** to be a *Leader of Yourself.*

INVENTORY OF TOTAL YOU

The next step is to inventory the total you—your talents, your relationships, your surroundings, your personality, your values, and your experiences. Reflect on and fill in each of these headings. Don't embellish, don't be modest—be honest!

TALENTS

• _____

• _____

• _____

• _____

• _____

• _____

• _____

• _____

• _____

• _____

RELATIONSHIPS

- _____
- _____
- _____
- _____
- _____
- _____
- _____
- _____
- _____
- _____

SURROUNDINGS

- _____
- _____
- _____
- _____
- _____
- _____
- _____

- _____
- _____
- _____

PERSONALITY

- _____
- _____
- _____
- _____
- _____
- _____
- _____
- _____
- _____
- _____

VALUES

- _____
- _____

- _____
- _____
- _____
- _____
- _____
- _____
- _____
- _____

EXPERIENCES

- _____
- _____
- _____
- _____
- _____
- _____
- _____
- _____
- _____
- _____

A *Leader of Yourself* makes the best use of skills, talents, relationships, surroundings, personality, and experiences. In order to bring this to fruition, you need to have a clear understanding of who you are. Now that you have completed this inventory, you can begin to master the skill of **Embracing a Commitment**.

COMMITMENT TO SELF

The first and most vital commitment is commitment to self. This commitment demands that you maximize the use of your talents, personality, skills, and experiences to become a total individual. Only when you have fully developed your commitment to self will your other commitments be able to reach their greatest potential.

EGOCENTRIC AND EGOTISTIC BEHAVIOR

Do not confuse commitment to self with egocentric or egotistic behavior. These two behaviors are completely different than commitment to self. In demonstrating egocentric behavior, a person reveals a belief that life rotates around him or her and everything he or she does is for his or her good and desires.

A person demonstrating egotistic behavior believes he or she is better than anyone else. He or she has a skewed opinion of himself or herself. Both of these behaviors draw energy from others for selfish reasons. These are two very different behaviors. Both of these behaviors reflect the need to gain skills to develop commitment to self.

*•ONE PERSON IS NOT BETTER THAN ANOTHER—
EACH PERSON IS JUST DIFFERENT•*

COMMITMENT TO RELATIONSHIPS

Commitment to relationships probably epitomizes the most commonly held perception of commitment. People may use the word commitment interchangeably with marriage or an exclusive relationship. Certainly, the selection of a lifelong partner is one of the most significant commitments a person makes. This commitment is not to be taken lightly or without serious thought and reflection. You have to possess a strong commitment to self as an "I" before you can participate in a healthy relationship as a "we."

This relationship, however, is only one of many different relationships that each person encounters. Others include relationships with friends, family, colleagues, teachers, workers, and service employees.

COMMITMENT TO A CHILD

When you bring a child into your life, you are making a commitment to parenthood. Your commitment is to nurture, guide, care for, and teach your child to the best of your ability with all the love, support, respect and skill you possess. Many times that commitment may mean sacrificing material things to provide for your child. You may miss vacations to spend quality time with your children.

•IF YOU'RE A PARENT—YOU'RE A PARENT FOR THE LIFE OF YOUR CHILD•

One time when I was working as a school principal, my son was in a kindergarten play. In order to get to his performance, I had to reschedule three meetings to late afternoon and then work an extra night to complete a project report.

It was a 45 minute drive and the traffic was horrendous. The parking lot was full so I had to park a dis-

tance away and run to the building. I walked into the kindergarten room just as the children took their places. All the children wore bear masks that they had made. The boys had bow ties and the girls had hair bows.

My son was watching the door and he waved as I entered. I stood in the back of the room totally out of breath. The play started. It lasted six minutes. The children read a poem about Winnie the Pooh. A little boy stood up and in a quiet voice said, "Winnie." A little girl stood and said, "the," followed by my son, who said, "Pooh." That was the extent of his performance.

I applauded and then offered my congratulations to my son on his wonderful performance. The children returned to their lessons and I hurriedly raced back to school to my meetings. I laughed at my expectations. I was glad I had been there. I often wonder if he remembers saying, "Pooh." I always will. I was glad I was there for his debut.

Of all the commitments we make, the commitment to parenthood carries the most awesome responsibility. It also carries unsurpassed joy, fantastic rewards, and unbelievable pride. When the going gets tough, you may need to review your initial commitment to being a parent. You agreed to a lifelong commitment. Dig deep into that PERSONAL TREASURE CHEST for strength, WIDEN YOUR PERSPECTIVES, find new CLASSROOMS OF LEARNING, SET REALISTIC GOALS, and give constant love to that child. In other words improve your skills—be a *Leader of Your Child*. The results will be amazing. It is your responsibility. You assumed that responsibility when you made the commitment to bring a child into your life.

COMMITMENT TO PARENTS

A commitment to parents becomes more and more critical as people live longer. This commitment includes guaranteeing good medical care, providing love, and insuring personal security for parents as they grow old. Medical researchers have successfully increased the probability of a longer life span. They have assumed that responsibility. It is our responsibility to improve the quality of life for our senior citizens. It is our responsibility to assure quality of life for our parents.

COMMITMENT TO A CAREER

This type of commitment is necessary for your success, for the survival of business, and ultimately for the economic prosperity of our society. When you approach work with a sincere commitment, you can use all your energy to do your best. Thus, you will not miss work unless it is absolutely unavoidable because you know you are an integral part of the team.

If, for example, you are in the restaurant business—your responsibility to be at work is the same whether you are the owner or the dishwasher. You need to complete your assigned duties in the total operation or someone else on the team has to carry an increased work load. When each person honors his or her commitment to perform at the highest level, the total operation runs much smoother and becomes a successful business ready to compete with any other business in the same profession or industry.

COMMITMENT TO A CAUSE

For those interested in this type of commitment, there are many groups anxiously awaiting your participation. You can become involved in such worthy causes as protecting endangered species or the rain forest, environmental issues, the crusade against domestic violence, programs for children, or working with substance abuse victims.

These commitments call for different levels of involvement including endorsement, stamping envelopes, distributing fliers, walking in peaceful demonstrations, or donating time or money. These causes, such as the fight against AIDS or the protection of animal rights, have different goals and target different populations. Make sure the one you select is one that endorses your common beliefs, thus assuring your full support—that is commitment.

COMMITMENT TO CIVIC WORK

This commitment has a whole range of opportunities, such as beautification efforts; service on committees, boards, and commissions; working in political campaigns; writing letters of support for ordinances, zoning, and laws; or holding public office. Civic work is probably one of the most needed and yet many people find it distasteful because of the political overtones.

However, the only way to reverse the negative feelings and restore confidence in government is to become involved at some level for a designated period of time. This is a crucial time for government as qualified people will soon refuse to step forward to assume leadership roles at any level.

COMMITMENT TO SERVICE AND CHARITABLE ORGANIZATIONS

When we think of volunteer work, usually this form of commitment comes to mind. Again, there is the opportunity to be involved in many different types of organizations such as hospitals, churches, schools, and service clubs. These organizations depend on volunteers to help supplement the frequently limited staff. There are many different levels of involvement as well as a wide variety of tasks.

Since I had been an assistant girl scout leader, I was willing to serve as a girl scout cookie chairman—a role that filled our garage with the smell of sugar. I didn't eat one cookie that year as I was nauseated by the overpowering scent.

Serving as a fund-raiser for a high school drill team, I stored and cataloged Christmas greens that were dead and shriveled upon arrival.

For three years in a row I was room mother for the kindergarten class and had that wonderful red punch spilled all over my white tennis shoes. I learned not to wear white tennis shoes after the second year .

As a soccer mother, I cut dozens of oranges into wedges for snacks and poured many glasses of fruit juice, followed by the picking up of the orange peels and cups after each time out.

One time as a religion teacher in an after school program for public school children, I had 91 children and all other teachers sick. The sisters, who were playing volleyball, refused to end their game to help. I turned over the key to the assistant pastor, who then had 90 children to supervise and instruct.

When I was a school carnival worker who manned the cotton-candy booth, I had cotton-candy in my hair and ears for days after the event. I manned the goldfish booth where parents prayed their children wouldn't get a fish and children prayed for a new pet. I manned the dart-toss booth where nary a balloon was hit but everything else in the booth was. I also played chef and manned the hamburger grill, soda pop dispenser, and even the Indian fry bread stand.

And when I sold fireworks in a booth, I prayed no one would toss a lighted match.

I always wondered where the rest of the parents were. There was always a small core of workers. In retrospect, I wonder how hard we really tried to get others involved. We didn't demand help—it really was easier to gripe while doing everything ourselves. We worked hard and had a lot of fun.

How many times have you been involved in a youth

organization where there is always a small group responsible for accomplishing all the tasks but a large group who drop their children off for the activity? Why does this situation repeat itself over and over?

Organizations have not yet found ways to involve more parents. Organizations can teach skills that will allow more parents to be involved. It is not only a matter of limited participation but perhaps also a matter of control by the small group. This needs to be broadened, particularly in youth organizations.

COMMITMENT TO PETS

People adopt dogs, cats, rabbits, rodents, and other pets and make them part of their family. Along with adoption goes the commitment to take care of them. Failure to follow through on this responsibility is cruel. If you choose to have an animal, then make sure you are committed to its well-being, including feeding, providing medical care, playing with, and protecting the animal.

We always were a family who had many animals—dogs, cats, rabbits, hamsters, gerbils, rats, mice, guinea pig, turtles, lizards, snakes, fish and for one day, a tortoise. Each of these animals generated many wonderful stories, but my favorite is about Myron.

Myron was a friendly white rat who was a wonderful pet. We paid fifty-nine cents for him and enjoyed him immensely. He developed a tumor after a couple of years. We took him to the vet who removed the tumor for fifty dollars. He called our son to report that Myron was in recovery and doing nicely. Myron came home healthy and full of life.

About a year later, Myron developed another tumor and we again took him to the vet, who removed the second tumor for another fifty dollars. This time Myron didn't survive the trauma of the operation. When I called to thank the vet for his kindness toward my son, he told me we should be thankful because Myron had lived two years more than his life expectancy.

COMMITMENT TO HOBBIES OR SPORTS

Commitment to a hobby or sport can satisfy many different needs: pleasure, physical fitness, interest, social, or as an outlet for talent. These commitments are usually for longer periods of time and may carry an intense level of commitment, such as participation on an athletic team.

Think about the commitment Olympic athletes make to their sport—it is total. Many give up normal childhood activities in order to dedicate themselves to hours of intense practice, workouts, skill building, and competition. This commitment also holds true for those who serve as players and coaches in youth programs, high school, college sports, and adult sports.

For over thirty years, my husband was a dedicated softball player and coach. He coached one of the first McDonalds-sponsored softball teams. Whenever we moved to a new state, he would sign on with a new team. Soon he would be coach. It was in his blood.

He used to get into heated arguments with umpires and was ejected from many games. I spent many hours sitting on wood or cement bleachers, on the grass, or in the dirt to support his teams.

One time he was knocked out running between second and third base. He had a serious concussion but didn't miss a game. He broke his hand, suffered separated shoulders, sprained ankles, and a broken nose, but nothing stopped him from playing and coaching.

The memory of one particular occasion brings a smile to my face. He was sliding into home plate to score the winning run in the final game of a tournament. The catcher, who weighed over 300 pounds, fell on him. He was knocked out, but his hand was on the plate. The team won and we celebrated before going to the emergency room. Commitment even while unconscious.

SHORT-TERM, LONG -TERM AND LIFETIME COMMITMENTS

There is a big difference in short-term, long-term, and lifetime commitments. They each require a different time investment. In order to be able to commit to a project, relationship, idea, job, or cause, it is necessary to determine the expected time commitment. Many times we get into a commitment and it becomes more involved than we originally thought. At that point, there needs to be a reassessment of the commitment. Do not just aimlessly give more and more time. When you take time to review your initial commitment, you can determine whether you want to continue. Just do this analysis consciously while considering all factors.

Short-term examples might include political campaigns, charity fund-raisers, involvement in causes and service organizations, organization committee work, classes, training, vacations, jobs, and relationships.

Long-term examples might include relationships, jobs, charity work, involvement in causes and service organizations, organization leadership positions, church, school, and training programs.

Lifetime commitments include family relationships, marriage, and parenthood. They may also include professions, church, hobbies, and volunteer work.

LEVELS OF COMMITMENT

There are different levels of commitment. Remember: one is not better than the other—each commitment is just different! All commitments are not alike. A good example is the one concerning breakfast. The chicken makes a different commitment than the pig. The chicken gives an egg but the pig gives a total commitment—the bacon. When determining the size of your commitment refer back to this example. Which are you giving?

OVERCOMMITMENT

A word of caution: do not overcommit. When you overcommit to organizations, causes, hobbies, or your work, you make it difficult to fulfill your other commitments. Sometimes your neglected commitments may even include your spouse or children. It is not only difficult but many times impossible to honor your commitment and fulfill your obligations when you become stretched so thin. It is far better to say no than to fail the relationship, the group, or the organization. This is a big concern. Too many commitments can lead to a breakdown in the family and poor parenting.

CHOOSING COMMITMENTS

When you have chosen an important person, activity, job, or interest in your life, you are ready to make a commitment. At this point you are determined to pursue your commitment with passion, vigor, and a high energy level.

Take time to analyze your choice. Look at your vision for that commitment. It is difficult to make a commitment without seeing the big picture of where your involvement is heading. You can only know what questions to ask if you have an idea of the big picture of the commitment. This encourages you to assess your skills to see if there is a match between you and your chosen commitment. It is important to see how your commitment fits into the big picture so that your involvement can be effective, meaningful, and rewarding.

For example, if you are talking about a commitment to marriage or an exclusive relationship, describe what you want for yourself and your partner. Is that what your partner wants? If it is a commitment to a job, examine the mission of the company. How do you fit in with the mission? What can be your contribution to the success of the company? If it is a commitment to an organization, review the goals of the organization. Can you support them? If you cannot, look for another organization which you are more comfortable supporting.

These are all questions that require answers prior to making a commitment. Choose something you like so that your interest will sustain your involvement. Every time you make a commitment to something, you need to know that your time and efforts will be productive.

•TIME IS YOUR MOST IMPORTANT RESOURCE•

•TIME CANNOT BE PURCHASED•

•TIME CANNOT BE SLOWED DOWN•

•TIME CANNOT BE RELIVED•

•DON'T WASTE IT•

DIFFICULTY IN COMMITMENTS

Too many times a commitment seems like a heavy burden. When you are having trouble with a commitment, you need to examine why you are having this difficulty. You could have failed to do an effective analysis prior to making the commitment. Hence, your ideas, values, and interests do not match. You could have ventured into a commitment for which you do not possess the necessary skills and thus you are not equipped to handle the responsibility. Then that commitment becomes difficult for you.

The most serious example of this is parenthood. We often hear the phrase, "Babies having babies." This is a very real problem for our society. Young people who have babies try to do their best but many times their effort and good intentions cannot overcome the lack of parenting and commitment skills.

When you find yourself in a commitment that is difficult and it is not possible to extricate yourself, your solution lies in defining the skills you need to learn. Return to the nine skills previously listed. Read them in depth. Do an inventory of yourself. Determine what skills you need. Remember, skills:

•CAN BE LEARNED•

•CAN BE IMPROVED•

•CAN BE PRACTICED•

•CAN BE REFINED•

•CAN BE MASTERED•

FULFILLING COMMITMENTS FULFILLS LIFE

A *Leader of Yourself* is able to embrace commitments at the highest level because the necessary skills have been mastered. We are at a time in our society when there appears to be a lack of responsibility. Perhaps there are a few generations who have not faced responsibility with all the intensity possible. This is the time to start—one by one, commitment by commitment.

CHOOSE COMMITMENTS

CAREFULLY,

THEN EMBRACE THEM!

LESSONS

- Make a list of your present commitments. Categorize them as to kinds, level of involvement, and time allocation required.

- Make a list of additional commitments anticipated during the next year.

- Review your present commitments as to success, effectiveness, and time allocation.

- Prioritize your commitments as to absolute need, interests, pleasure, service, and fulfillment.

- Identify the skills required to embrace fully the commitments you have selected to fulfill your life.

Commencement

TIME TO BEGIN

As we approach the new millennium, it is time to commence our efforts to develop leadership skills in each person. The abandonment of learning and our failure to develop the mind, heart, and spirit of our people must stop. This path has brought us to a violent society troubled by family breakdown, prejudice, distrust of government, illiteracy, child abuse, hate crimes, domestic violence, substance abuse, and terrorism. Examples of our dysfunctional society are publicized daily on talk shows and news programs, and reflected in movies, television shows, and the lyrics of our songs.

The popular solutions to our problems include welfare reform, more police, stricter laws, more prisons, sophisticated security systems for homes, businesses, and cars, militias, and of course mace, pepper spray, and guns for protection.

The viable solution to our problems is to develop, nurture, and maximize leadership skills in each person. Until each person is prepared as a leader, current problems will intensify and current solutions will continue to be ineffective. One of our biggest challenges is to negate the myth that leadership belongs only to a few distinguished people in politics, the military, or the world of business, sports, entertainment, and religion, or those glorified by the media.

PEOPLE ARE THE MOST VALUABLE ASSET

Our world is not about things. It is not about buildings. It is not about technology. It is first and foremost about people. Yes, people interact with things, buildings, and technology. But the key point is that people interact. Things, buildings, and technology have no use without people. People have use without things, buildings, and technology.

When each person becomes a leader, people will be able to work together for common goals. Now, more than ever, this is needed in society. We have major problems that need solving. Things, buildings, and technology cannot solve these problems. People, with their—
talents,
creativity,
dedication,
enthusiasm,
humor,
and heart,
can solve any problem that arises. Things, buildings, and technology do not share these necessary ingredients.

YOU MUST LEAD THE WAY

Each of the **ten skills** necessary to become a *Leader of Yourself* can be learned. To learn them you must intentionally focus on them. The excitement you experience as a **lifelong learner** creates a desire to WIDEN YOUR PERSPECTIVES, expand your CLASSROOMS OF LEARNING, continue to grow, and develop your skills.

It becomes a living passion. It explodes the myth that when your formal education is complete, you stop learning. In fact, this is when you open your vistas, learn at an exponential rate, and gain confidence in your ability to learn what you choose to learn. Most formal education does not allow for your choice of interests. In all my formal education—over twenty-two years—I had four elective classes. It has only been as a lifelong learner that I have ventured slowly into the sciences and arts.

The joy and uplifting feeling that comes from maintaining a **positive attitude** builds your confidence so that you know you can conquer the world and tackle any problem with your best effort. A positive attitude draws positive people to you and brightens your whole environment.

When you internalize the skill of **love** you create an inner peace, which is best stated in a wonderful saying I keep on my desk: *A smile is put on your face to let the world know your heart is at home.* When your heart is at home, you exude a calmness that attracts other loving people.

Reclaiming your **personal power** gives you a great feeling of being in control of yourself. It gives you strength to break addictions and to be in charge of your own life. It also helps with your relationships.

Creating a **supportive environment** is fun. It makes you look at your surroundings with a microscope. It guides your purchases as well as your selection of friends. It also is a skill that helps your relationships.

When you understand your PERSONAL FILTRATION SYSTEM, a whole new world of **communication** opens to you. You begin to observe the power of communication and to find new ways to express yourself. You also have a better understanding of what other people are communicating to you.

The skill of **focusing your life** provides an organization and sense of order to your life. It helps you have a handle on the elusive time that slips by so fast. It is a good feeling to set realistic and target goals that you can achieve. It is a great feeling when you make your goal.

Learning to fill your PERSONAL TREASURE CHEST will give you newfound strength, which is very comforting in times of stress and helps you grow from **adversity**. Replenishing the treasure chest allows you to savor the good times instead of taking them for granted.

The security and excitement that you can feel during times of change is the reward for learning to **adapt to the accelerated change** all around us. It is far more comfortable to be involved in the change than to be on the outside surrounded by fear.

Embracing a commitment gives us a wonderful feeling of purpose. It makes our life meaningful by allowing us to be passionate about what we are doing. This feeling is irreplaceable. When you feel the rush of a commitment, there is no comparison. Whether it is running a marathon, sewing a dress, decorating a room, teaching a child, growing fresh vegetables in your own garden, performing in a play, being a caring mother, or writing a book, the passion of a commitment gives us an exhilarated feeling that money cannot buy.

•A LEADER OF YOURSELF HAS A VISION OF LIFE'S PURPOSE•

•A LEADER OF YOURSELF PUTS THIS VISION TO WORK THROUGH CAREFULLY SELECTED COMMITMENTS•

DO YOUR LESSONS: PRACTICE—PRACTICE—PRACTICE

Choose one lesson for each skill and begin to move along your path toward being a *Leader of Yourself.*

•SET YOUR OWN PACE•

•DON'T COMPETE WITH OTHERS•

•DEVELOP A PLAN•

If you have a friend or family member working to develop leadership skills at the same time, have conversations.

•DISCUSS THE CONCEPTS•

•DISCUSS STRATEGIES•

•DISCUSS SUCCESSES•

Find encouragement from others, but most importantly build encouragement in yourself. Have fun with your lessons. Have you noticed that people who cry a lot rarely laugh?

•LAUGHTER IS THE MUSIC OF THE SOUL•

As you master each skill, you will feel excitement and purpose at the same time you achieve peace and serenity. This is a wonderful combination. This is what awaits a *Leader of Yourself*.

SKILLED INDIVIDUALS MAKE GROUPS SUCCESSFUL

The success of families, businesses, schools, organizations, government agencies, and other groups is dependent on the contribution of each individual member. The contribution of each individual member is based on the skill of each member to be a leader.

The success of the family is dependent on the contribution of each member of the family. If each member is a leader, the family will be functional, supportive and successful.

Likewise, an organization is the total result of each individual affiliated with the organization. Therefore, if each individual in the organization becomes a leader, the organization becomes a leader in its industry, profession, or field of interest.

So also is society the total result of each individual. When each individual is a leader, society will be a positive, nurturing, productive, and peaceful entity.

Society is continually attempting to redefine values or quality of life. There are T-shirts and bumper stickers that say, "He who gathers the most toys in life wins." Yet with increased signs of hatred, violence, crime, breakdown of families, child abuse, and substance abuse, it is apparent that this gathering of things does not bring happiness, security, fulfillment, or "winning." Each person must be an effective leader for this society to enjoy a good quality of life.

EDUCATION—LEAD THE WAY

Make education as big-time as sports. Have you been around a Superbowl or World Series? Have you experienced the excitement of the Olympics? Have you ever seen a similar scale of hype for thinking and learning? Have you ever seen our society become enamored with educating people?

Educating people does not mean that all learning takes place formally in school. Schools must change dramatically. For some students, there is more learning in an arcade than in a classroom. Some schools are out of touch with the needs of students. School systems are mired in institutional problems. Each individual must demand and receive the opportunity to learn, to become educated, and to be proud to be a learner.

BUILD A SOCIETY OF LEARNERS

You are one of the people in society. Each of us is one of the people in society. Each of us is like a piece of a puzzle with society being the total puzzle. Each piece is needed to fit in place to complete the puzzle. Each of us with different experiences and personalities, different perspectives, different shapes, colors, and edges, must come together to make the puzzle a masterpiece.

There must be a new spirit, a spirit that demands the development of our greatest resource—our people. There must be a massive swell encouraging each person to be a learner.

•EACH PERSON MUST BE INVOLVED IN LEARNING•

•EACH PERSON MUST COUNT•

If we do not build a society of learners, we will all pay the price and it will be expensive beyond imagination. Time is running out.

•START TODAY TO BE A LEADER OF YOURSELF•

•START TODAY TO BUILD A SOCIETY OF LEARNERS•

Once you master that role, you can become *Leader of Your Children.* Then our children will learn leadership skills so they can live in a peaceful and harmonious world where people are recognized as the greatest resource in the society.

•ENJOY YOUR JOURNEY MASTERING THE TEN SKILLS•

•CELEBRATE YOUR PROGRESS•

•BE PROUD TO BE THE LEADER OF YOURSELF•

LET US COMMENCE!